SOCIETY FOR OLD TESTAMENT STUDY

MONOGRAPH SERIES

GENERAL EDITOR

J. A. EMERTON

2

# GIBEON AND ISRAEL

THE ROLE OF GIBEON AND THE GIBEONITES IN THE POLITICAL AND RELIGIOUS HISTORY OF EARLY ISRAEL

*Other books in the series:*

R. N. Whybray *The Heavenly Counsellor in Isaiah xl 13–14: A study of the sources of the theology of Deutero-Isaiah.*

# GIBEON AND ISRAEL

## THE ROLE OF GIBEON AND THE GIBEONITES IN THE POLITICAL AND RELIGIOUS HISTORY OF EARLY ISRAEL

JOSEPH BLENKINSOPP

*Associate Professor of Theology in the University of Notre Dame, Indiana*

CAMBRIDGE
AT THE UNIVERSITY PRESS
1972

Published by the Syndics of the Cambridge University Press
Bentley House, 200 Euston Road, London NW1 2DB
American Branch: 32 East 57th Street, New York, N.Y.10022

Library of Congress Catalogue Card Number: 74–171672

ISBN: 0 521 08368 0

Printed in Great Britain
at the University Printing House, Cambridge
(Brooke Crutchley, University Printer)

# CONTENTS

# PREFACE

The following monograph grew out of a long-standing interest in the Gibeonite problem, especially in its relations to the cultic history of early Israel. It soon becomes apparent to anyone studying the Old Testament tradition with respect to the Gibeonite cities and their inhabitants that many larger questions are involved: the obscure history of the ark before its transfer to Jerusalem, the role of the local sanctuaries, the political and religious significance of Saul, the early history of Benjamin before its assimilation into the Davidic state system. Discussion of these larger issues in this context is not of course new; but it is hoped that a new look at what may fairly be called the Gibeonite problem will contribute to our knowledge of early Israel, and in particular the obscure half-century which preceded the accession of David.

Some aspects of these issues were discussed in a paper read several years ago before the Catholic Biblical Association in London under the title 'The Enigma of Gibeon'. More directly, this study is based on a thesis submitted to the Faculty of Theology of the University of Oxford in fulfilment of requirements for the degree of Doctor of Philosophy. The present study is, in effect, an abbreviated and revised version of that thesis which is catalogued under the title 'Gibeon and the Gibeonites from the Settlement to Solomon'.

I wish to express my thanks and appreciation to the many who, over the last few years, have helped me with their comments and criticism. I owe a particular debt to the Revd G. Henton Davies, Principal of Regent's Park College, who supervised my work at Oxford and commented on it in detail. During the same period I also profited much from the critical acumen of the Revd Professor H. F. D. Sparks, Chairman of the Faculty of Theology. Professor James B. Pritchard of the University of Pennsylvania, whose excavations at el-Jîb have placed all Old Testament scholars in his debt, took time off from a busy career to read the present work in manuscript and make valuable comments. Discussions at an early stage with the Revd Professors Joseph Coppens and Henri Cazelles proved invaluable and thanks are also due to Professor G. E. Mendenhall of the University of Michigan who kindly sent me a copy of an unpublished paper together with comments on an important aspect of the Gibeonite problem. I wish, finally, to express appreciation to the Revd Professor J. A. Emerton, editor of the present monograph series, who accepted the manuscript for publication.

JOSEPH BLENKINSOPP

*Notre Dame, Indiana*
*December 1971*

# ABBREVIATIONS

| | |
|---|---|
| *A.A.S.O.R.* | *Annual of the American Schools of Oriental Research* |
| *A.J.S.L.* | *American Journal of Semitic Languages and Literatures* |
| *Anal.Or.* | *Analecta Orientalia* |
| *A.N.E.T.* | *Ancient Near Eastern Texts relating to the Old Testament*, ed. J. B. Pritchard, 2nd edn, Princeton, 1955 |
| *A.O.* | *Archiv Orientální* |
| A.T.D. | Das Alte Testament Deutsch |
| *B.A.* | *The Biblical Archaeologist* |
| *B.A.S.O.R.* | *Bulletin of the American Schools of Oriental Research* |
| B.D.B. | F. Brown, S. R. Driver, C. A. Briggs, *A Hebrew and English Lexicon of the Old Testament*, Oxford, 1907 |
| *B.H.* | R. Kittel, *Biblia Hebraica* (3rd edn) |
| *Bib.* | *Biblica* |
| *B.I.E.S.* | *Bulletin of the Israel Exploration Society* |
| *B.J.P.E.S.* | *Bulletin of the Jewish Palestine Exploration Society* |
| *B.J.R.L.* | *Bulletin of the John Rylands Library* |
| B.W.A.N.T. | Beiträge zur Wissenschaft vom Alten und Neuen Testament |
| B.Z.A.W. | Beihefte zur *Zeitschrift für die alttestamentliche Wissenschaft* |
| *C.A.H.* | *The Cambridge Ancient History* (2nd edn, 1963; vols. I and II in fascicle) |
| *C.B.Q.* | *The Catholic Biblical Quarterly* |
| *Comm.Viat.* | *Communio Viatorum* |
| *E.T.L.* | *Ephemerides Theologicae Lovanienses* |
| E.Tr. | English Translation |
| *H.U.C.A.* | *Hebrew Union College Annual* |
| I.C.C. | International Critical Commentary |
| *I.D.B.* | *The Interpreter's Dictionary of the Bible*, New York and Nashville, 1962 |
| *I.E.J.* | *Israel Exploration Journal* |

| | |
|---|---|
| *J.A.O.S.* | *Journal of the American Oriental Society* |
| *J.B.L.* | *Journal of Biblical Literature* |
| *J.C.S.* | *Journal of Cuneiform Studies* |
| *J.N.E.S.* | *Journal of Near Eastern Studies* |
| *J.P.O.S.* | *Journal of the Palestine Oriental Society* |
| *J.Q.R.* | *Jewish Quarterly Review* |
| *J.S.S.* | *Journal of Semitic Studies* |
| *J.T.S.* | *Journal of Theological Studies* |
| *K.S.* | A. Alt, *Kleine Schriften zur Geschichte des Volkes Israel*, 3 vols., Munich, 1953–9 |
| M.T. | The Massoretic Text |
| *Norsk T.T.* | *Norsk Teologisk Tidsskrift* |
| *O.L.Z.* | *Orientalistische Literaturzeitung* |
| *Orient.* | *Orientalia* |
| *O.S.* | *Oudtestamentische Studiën* |
| *P.E.Q.* | *Palestine Exploration Quarterly* (earlier *Palestine Exploration Fund Quarterly Statement*) |
| *P.J.B.* | *Palästinajahrbuch des deutschen evangelischen Instituts für Altertumswissenschaft des Heiligen Landes zu Jerusalem* |
| *R.A.* | *Revue d'Assyriologie et d'Archéologie orientale* |
| *R.B.* | *Revue Biblique* |
| *R.E.S.* | *Revue des Études Sémitiques* |
| *Rev.Bib.* | *Revista Bíblica* |
| *R.G.G.* | *Die Religion in Geschichte und Gegenwart* (3rd edn) |
| *R.H.A.* | *Revue Hittite et Asianique* |
| *R.H.R.* | *Revue de l'Histoire des Religions* |
| R.S.V. | The Revised Standard Version |
| S.A.T. | Die Schriften des Alten Testaments |
| S.D.B. | Supplement to *Dictionnaire de la Bible* |
| *St.Th.* | *Studia Theologica*, Lund |
| S.V.T. | Supplements to *Vetus Testamentum* |
| Symm. | Symmachus |
| Syr. | Syriac version |
| *T.L.Z.* | *Theologische Literaturzeitung* |
| *T.Z.* | *Theologische Zeitschrift* |
| *V.D.* | *Verbum Domini* |

| | |
|---|---|
| *V.T.* | *Vetus Testamentum* |
| *Z.A.* | *Zeitschrift für Assyriologie* |
| *Z.A.W.* | *Zeitschrift für die alttestamentliche Wissenschaft* |
| *Z.D.M.G.* | *Zeitschrift der deutschen Morgenländischen Gesellschaft* |
| *Z.D.P.V.* | *Zeitschrift des deutschen Palästina-Vereins* |
| *Z.K.W.K.L.* | *Zeitschrift für kirchliche Wissenschaft und kirchliches Leben* |
| *Z.T.K.* | *Zeitschrift für Theologie und Kirche* |

CHAPTER I

# GIBEON AND ITS CITIES

Since a study of the role of Gibeon and the Gibeonites in the history of Israel from the Settlement to Solomon has to rely almost exclusively on what has been preserved in the Old Testament we could do no better than begin with a survey of this material. The list of four Gibeonite cities with which Israel entered into treaty-relationship (Joshua ix.17) warns us that such a study cannot be confined to the city of Gibeon. The gentilic occurs in the plural only in the account of the ritual execution of the Saulites (2 Sam. xxi.1–14) where it refers, in all probability, to the inhabitants of some if not all of the four cities. Elsewhere individuals from the city of Gibeon are mentioned: Ishmaiah (1 Chron. xii.4), Hananiah ben-Azzur a prophet (Jer. xxviii.1), Melatiah (Neh. iii.7). These represent a type of name which appears to have been common at Gibeon during the divided monarchy since several of the same formation have turned up in the excavation of el-Jîb, including two Hananiahs.[1] 2 Sam. xxiii.37 (=1 Chron. xi.39) refers to a Beerothite named Naharai who was the armour-bearer of Joab and one of the Thirty, David's *corps d'élite*. The two assassins of Ishbaal, Baanah and Rechab sons of Rimmon (2 Sam. iv.2), also came from the same city. We may recall, finally, that the martyr-prophet Uriah ben-Shemaiah, a contemporary of Jeremiah (Jer. xxvi.20), was a native of Kiriath-jearim, the fourth of the Gibeonite cities.

The place-name *giḇʿôn* occurs some forty times in M.T., covering the period from the treaty to the exile and beyond. It is the first mentioned of the four with whose inhabitants the treaty was made and is described as 'a great city, like one of the royal cities', greater than Ai and renowned for its warriors (Joshua x.2). It features in the Benjaminite city-list (Joshua xviii.25) and was one of the Levitical cities allocated to the descendants of Aaron (Joshua xxi.17). The execution of the descendants of Saul handed over to the Gibeonites by David is described as taking place 'at Gibeon on the mountain of the Lord' (2 Sam. xxi.6).[2] Other fateful events which took place at Gibeon during the same reign were the meeting between Abner and Joab and the ensuing hostilities (2 Sam. ii.12–24),[3] the assassination of Amasa (iii.30; xx.8) and David's final victory over the Philistines (v.25; cf. 1 Chron. xiv.16).[4] Solomon visited the Gibeon sanctuary at the beginning of his reign and it was here, at 'the great high place', that he was favoured with an oracle of good augury (1 Kings iii.4–5; ix.2; cf. 2 Chron. i.3, 13). It was by 'the great pool which is in Gibeon' that Johanan came upon the assassins of Gedaliah (Jer. xli.12, 16), and we learn from Neh. vii.25 that Gibeonites were among those who returned from exile in Babylon. Finally, we should mention the important role of Gibeon in the Chronicler's cultic history (1 Chron. xvi.39; xxi.29) and the topographical genealogies towards the beginning of his work (viii.29; ix.35).

A glance at this rapid survey reveals a rather strange fact which might seem to call for explanation. Gibeon is first mentioned in the account of the treaty shortly after the Settlement and thereafter during the early part of David's reign and that of his successor down to the building of the temple. During the long period of the Judges and the reign of Saul, however, there is not a single occurrence of the name in M.T., despite the fact that it is precisely at this time that we would expect this 'great city' and 'great high place' to have played a significant role in the political and religious history of Israel. This gap in the historical tradition has focussed attention on the frequent textual confusion between *giḇʿôn* and similar forms, notably the place-names *giḇʿāh* and *geḇaʿ* and the substantive *giḇʿāh* (hill), with or without the article. Both of the place-names occur in Benjamin within whose boundaries Gibeon also was located. Benjaminite Gibeah is variously described as 'Gibeah which belongs to Benjamin' (Judges xix.14; xx.4), 'Gibeah of Benjamin' (1 Sam. xiii.2, 15; xiv.16), 'Gibeah of Saul' (1 Sam. xi.4; xv.34; 2 Sam. xxi.6) or simply Gibeah. From the context, the 'Gibeah of Elohim' of 1 Sam. x.5 must be identical with the Gibeah of x.10 since it was there that Saul was to meet, and did meet, the band of prophets. It is by no means certain, however, that the place referred to is Saul's city since we could, with equal probability, translate 'the hill of God' or 'the most high hill', thus leaving its precise location open. While there are very few cases, perhaps only two,[5] where we are obliged to emend M.T. to *giḇʿôn* on purely textual grounds, the silence of the tradition about Gibeon during this crucial period (Judges and Saul) has tempted many scholars to suppose that, in some instances at least, *haggiḇʿāh* has either replaced *giḇʿôn* or refers indirectly to it.[6] We shall have to evaluate these hypotheses in the course of this study.

Neither the place-name nor the gentilic occurs in any non-biblical text from the period under consideration. Gibeon is mentioned in a city-list from the time of Sheshonk I (945–924 B.C.) on the wall of the Amun temple at Karnak commemorating his invasion of Palestine, an event referred to in 1 Kings xiv.25.[7] Some thirty jar handles bearing the inscription *g b ʿ n* in the Phoenician lettering have been recovered from the site of el-Jîb, but these come from a period somewhere between the beginning of the seventh century and the Exile.[8]

We must now turn to the location of the Gibeonite cities listed in Joshua ix.17. We can conclude from the texts referred to earlier that Gibeon was in Benjamin (Joshua xviii.25), not more than a night's march from Gilgal near the Jordan (Joshua x.9; cf. ix.6–7, 16) and not too distant from the Philistine area (2 Sam. v.25, LXX). Noth deduces from 2 Sam. xx.8 that it must have lain on the main road north from Jerusalem, assuming that Abishai and Joab were heading due north to deal with the rebellion of Sheba and that the encounter with Amasa at Gibeon was fortuitous.[9] But in view of the fact that the city seems to have been favoured as a meeting place (cf. 2 Sam. ii.12ff.; Jer. xli.12, 16), it is equally possible that the encounter was pre-arranged for reasons not stated in the text. The Sheshonk list just referred to, in which we have the earliest non-biblical reference to the city, cannot be used with any confidence to determine the precise location of Gibeon. The cities are not listed necessarily in the topographical order of the Pharaoh's victorious progress northward and, in any case, the identification of at least two key place-names is uncertain.[10]

Later Jewish tradition is interested in Gibeon as one of the three loci of the Tent, and therefore of the *Shekinah*, before the building of the Temple. It does not, however, provide any help towards identifying the site. Josephus informs us that during the Civil War Cestius pitched his camp at Gibeon which was fifty (or perhaps forty) stadia from Jerusalem.[11] This would certainly be consistent with a location at el-Jîb and is confirmed by the evident strategic importance of Nebi Samwil about a mile away.[12] The *Onomasticon* of Eusebius places Gibeon on the road leading north out of Jerusalem, which led Alt to identify it first with Tell en-Naṣbeh and later, when this was ruled out by Badè's excavations at that site, with el-Bireh.[13] But not only is the interpretation of the *Onomasticon* uncertain at this point – Abel has argued against Alt that it is reconcilable with Josephus[14] – it also conflicts with other texts from the early Christian period which favour el-Jîb or Nebi Samwil. Jerome has preserved a statement of Paula to the effect that she saw Gibeon on her right as she was going up to Jerusalem, which would be consistent with a location at el-Jîb. Epiphanius refers to a summit which he calls ἡ Γαβαων, about eight miles from Jerusalem, the only one which could vie with the Mount of Olives in height.[15] This suggests that Nebi Samwil was known locally as Gibeon in the fourth century.

The accounts of pilgrims from about the fourth century to early modern times do not provide reliable guidance since it is uncertain to what extent, if at all, they rely on traditions independent of particular interpretations of the biblical material. Some of these accounts, such as the *Liber de Locis Sacris* of Peter the Deacon, betray in addition a rather confused knowledge of the relevant Old Testament texts.[16] We may add that attempts to locate one or other of the Gibeonite cities on the basis of the Madaba mosaic map bring us no closer to a solution.[17]

That controversy has raged for practically a century over the identification of Gibeon, there being at least three claimants among modern sites (el-Jîb, el-Bireh, Tell en-Naṣbeh), suggests that no clear and unanimous tradition has survived from the early Christian period. Visitors to Palestine in the early modern period tended to opt for either el-Jîb or Nebi Samwil (as Franz Ferdinand von Troilo in 1666 and Richard Pococke in 1738) but it was not until the historic visit of Edward Robinson in 1838 that this identification was supported with arguments.[18] Robinson spent only forty minutes at the site of el-Jîb on 8 May of that year and had probably reached this conclusion before setting out, mainly on the basis of the similarity between the ancient and modern place-names. We should note however that this argument is not without its difficulties, principally because of the absence of *'ayin* in the Arabic name and the long *i* in *j î b*.[19] At any rate, the claim of el-Jîb was widely accepted by scholars with an excellent knowledge of Palestinian topography even before the excavation of the site by J. B. Pritchard. As the results of the excavations began to come in, others who had been doubtful (Noth and Albright in particular) also accepted this identification.[20]

During the five seasons between 1956 and 1962 Professor Pritchard and his colleagues uncovered epigraphical evidence of names connected with Gibeon and some thirty jar handles bearing the inscription *g b ' n* in circumstances which strongly suggested that they were original to the site. *ḥ n n y h w* on one of the handles corresponds to the name of the Gibeonite prophet in Jer. xxviii. 1. *n r '* which occurs several times and which is, as Pritchard suggests, probably hypocoristic, is identical with the Neriah of Jer. xxxvi. 32 and may be compared with Ner in the Gibeonite 'genealogy' of the Chronicler (1 Chron. viii. 33; ix. 36). Pritchard suggests that the puzzling *g d r* in the frequently recurring *g b ' n g d r* refers to the place-name Gederah (1 Chron. xii. 5) probably to be identified with

Jedireh about half a mile north-east of el-Jîb.[21] That the jars originated at el-Jîb is established beyond reasonable doubt by the presence of stoppers and funnels which fit them, suggesting that the bottling was done at this 'Bordeaux of Palestine'.[22] In short, it may be maintained that the identification has been established beyond reasonable doubt.

Apart from positively identifying the site, the excavations at el-Jîb have given us disappointingly little information for the period corresponding to the end of Late Bronze and Iron I. The main problem is the absence of any significant evidence for the 'great city' which the biblical evidence would lead us to suppose existed towards the end of Late Bronze. Perhaps the site of the Late Bronze city lies elsewhere on the tell, only a relatively small area of which was excavated. What little evidence there is suggests that the city may have been enlarged and possibly resettled about this time. Pritchard dates the first city wall not later than ca. 1200 B.C. and the first stage of the vast hydraulic works may have been carried through about the same time.[23] Albright claims that this absence of evidence favours the view that Gibeon was an insignificant settlement attached to Jerusalem,[24] a possibility which we will examine at a later stage. Until we know definitely whether a Late Bronze city existed on the site, it will be unwise to make too much of *argumenta e silentio*.

The strategic importance of Gibeon, amply attested in the biblical record, is due not just to its high elevation and its situation on a major route from the Central Highlands to the Coastal Plain but to the abundance of its water supply. Jer. xli. 12 speaks of 'the great waters which are in Gibeon' and 2 Sam. ii. 13 more specifically of 'the pool (*bᵉrēḵāh*) of Gibeon'. This can no longer be identified with the reservoir north-east of the tell which dates from the Roman period. Pritchard tentatively identifies it with the great cylindrical cistern eighty-two feet deep discovered and cleared in 1956–7.[25] It might, however, be objected that this could hardly be called a *bᵉrēḵāh* and in any case it is inside the wall, whereas the single combat in 2 Sam. ii. 13–16 must have taken place outside the city limits, a conclusion suggested strongly by the name of the site, *ḥelqaṯ haṣṣūrîm*.[26]

'The great stone which is in Gibeon' (2 Sam. xx.8) has sometimes been identified with the altar upon which Solomon offered sacrifices as recorded in 1 Kings iii.4.[27] While this is hypothetical, it may find support in the reference to 'the great stone' set up by Saul after his victory over the Philistines. This constituted the first altar erected by him to Yahweh and was certainly in the Gibeonite region (1 Sam. xiv.33–5; cf. v.31). That the excavations have revealed no trace of a sanctuary or altar does not, of course, prove that the Gibeonites worshipped on Nebi Samwil but it would be in accord with this hypothesis. If, as will be proposed later, some Gibeonites served as cultic personnel at the Gibeonite high place, the appropriateness of the description 'hewers of wood and drawers of water' would, on the basis of this hypothesis, be beyond question. Nebi Samwil lies about a mile south of el-Jîb with an elevation above sea level of some 2,835 feet, more than 492 feet higher than el-Jîb. This would already suggest that this, the most imposing elevation north-west of Jerusalem, must have seemed an ideal site for religious worship. If any site in that part of Palestine may be described as 'the mountain' (2 Sam. xxi.9), 'the hill' (1 Sam. vii.1; 2 Sam. vi.3), or 'the great high place' (1 Kings iii.4) it would surely be Nebi Samwil.[28]

The second in the list of Gibeonite cities is Chephirah, also mentioned in connection with the list of repatriated Judahites after the Exile (Ezra ii.25 = Neh. vii.29). It too is attributed to Benjamin (Joshua xviii.26) and is generally identified with Tell Kefîreh less than five miles west of el-Jîb and north-north-west of Jerusalem.[29] Two of the Amarna letters were written by a certain Baʿalat-neše (*belit neše*) from somewhere north of Jerusalem in the vicinity of *a-ia-lu-na* (Aijalon) and *ṣa-ar-ḫa* (probably Sarʿa near Beth-shemesh);[30] and it has been suggested that this 'lady of the lions' wrote from the biblical city of Chephirah since *neše* (ideographically UR-MAḪ-MEŠ) corresponds to *kᵉpîrîm*.[31] If this is correct, we have here the only occurrence of any of the Gibeonite cities in the Amarna letters.

Beeroth ('Wells'), third in the list, is also Benjaminite (Joshua xviii.25) and according to Ezra ii.25=Neh. vii.29 was repopulated after the Exile. It is probably identical with the Berea of the Maccabean period (1 Macc. ix.4). Neither the biblical texts nor the reference to this city in the *Onomasticon* help us in locating it and its identification cannot be solved apart from the long-standing controversy about Gibeon and Mizpah. Earlier identification with either el-Jîb or Tell en-Naṣbeh has had to be abandoned after the excavations carried out by Pritchard and Badè respectively.[32] Kallai-Kleinmann places it at Nebi Samwil but this does not take account of the peculiar relations between this site and neighbouring el-Jîb.[33] From the time of Robinson, el-Bireh (more precisely, nearby Raš eṭ-Ṭahūne) has been the favourite claimant.[34] This site, about ten miles north of Jerusalem, is consistent with the biblical references, finds support in onomastic similarity (though this in itself is not enough) and has achieved a greater degree of probability with the elimination of its principal rivals.

We saw earlier that the Benjaminite Rimmon, father of Baanah and Rechab who assassinated Ishbaal, came from Beeroth (2 Sam. iv.2ff.). Following on this information the writer, or perhaps a later glossator, deemed it useful to add that Beeroth was a Benjaminite city and that its inhabitants fled to Gittaim where they were *gērîm* up to the time of writing. The situation of the city to which they fled continues to cause difficulty. The name occurs only here and in Neh. xi.33 where it is listed as Benjaminite. But Gittaim is the dual form of Gath, and in 1 Chron. vii.21 and viii.13 a Gath is mentioned which can only with great difficulty be identified with the well known Philistine city.[35] It would be reasonable therefore to advance the hypothesis that this Gath is identical with the Gittaim of 2 Sam. iv.3.[36] The question would then arise whether this Gath–Gittaim occurs elsewhere and whether, in particular, it may be identified with the Gath where Obed-edom lived in whose house the ark was left before its definitive transfer to Jerusalem (2 Sam. vi.10). This in its turn would lead to the interesting possibility that Obed-edom may have been of the Beerothite Gibeonites who fled to Gittaim and was still there in the early years of David's reign.[37] This, of course, can only be suggested, not proved. But it is at least more likely that he was a Gibeonite rather than a Philistine since, having just taken the ark from Philistine control (2 Sam. vi.1ff. following directly on v.25), it is highly unlikely that David would have given it back into the charge of a Philistine, even a holy Philistine. We must recall that the ark had just been removed from a Gibeonite city.

The note in 2 Sam. iv.2*b* gives no reason for the flight of the Beerothites, but in view of the fact that Beeroth was a Gibeonite city we may suggest that it was occasioned by the hostile action of Saul against this alien ethnic group. Evidence of such action against Gibeonites is found in 2 Sam. xxi.2, also in the form of an explanatory note, and may be suggested also for the inhabitants of Kiriath-jearim, as we shall see.

The last in the Gibeonite list and first in the post-exilic list is Kiriath-jearim.[38] The first problem which calls for discussion in connection with this city arises from the fact that it is the only one which is attributed to both Benjamin (Joshua xviii.28) and Judah (xv.16) and is located on the boundary of both tribes (xviii.14; xv.9). The position of Kiriath-jearim in the tribal boundary descriptions is particularly significant. A comparison between the two boundary lists (Joshua xv.5–9 and xviii.15–20), which are practically identical though in inverse order, will reveal the crucially important situation of this city. Not only does the Judahite–Benjaminite boundary *end* at Kiriath-jearim (Joshua xviii.14); it also forms the nodal point between the tribal territories of Judah, Benjamin and Dan, all of which are concerned in the movements of the ark prior to its 'translation' to Jerusalem. More specifically, the three stages of the ark's movement after its capture by the Philistines occur in inverse order in the Judah boundary list (Kiriath-jearim, Beth-shemesh, Ekron, Joshua xv.9*b*–11*a*), hence, by implication, in the direct order of the Benjaminite boundary list. This fact, which has so far gone unnoticed, may well provide an important clue to the interpretation of the early ark-narratives in 1–2 Sam.

It will be noticed that in the lists Kiriath-jearim is identified with Baalah (Joshua xv.9) or Kiriath-baal (xv.60; xviii.14) with which we may compare *ba'alê yehûḏāh* in 2 Sam. vi.2, interpreted by many as the point from which David set out in taking the ark to Jerusalem. In the parallel narrative of the Chronicler (1 Chron. xiii.6) this point is described as 'Baalah, that is, Kiriath-jearim which belongs to Judah', which appears to be a conflation of Joshua xv.9*b* and xviii.14. This would seem to lead to the conclusion that Kiriath-jearim was earlier known as Baalah, or some similar form, and that it first acquired its new name when it passed into Judahite hands.[39] Against this view, however, we should note that *qiryaṯ-* is a genuinely ancient form found in Syria and Palestine from at least Middle Bronze, *q r t* occurring more than once in Ugaritic and Punic texts.[40] We may add that the former names of Hebron and Debir were, respectively, Kiriath-arba (Joshua iv.15) and Kiriath-sepher (Joshua xv.15).[41] Moreover, the occurrence of both Mount Jearim and Mount Baalah in this section of the Judahite boundary description (Joshua xv.10–11) would rather suggest that Kiriath-jearim and Baalah were topographically distinct and that therefore the hybrid form Kiriath-baal was formed at a later redactional stage. We shall also see in a later chapter that it is not necessary and perhaps not even legitimate to interpret *ba'alê yehûḏāh* of 2 Sam. vi.2 as a place-name.

The only consensus which has so far emerged from the discussion of the date to be assigned to the city-lists is that they derive, in all probability, from an administrative measure carried out some time during the divided monarchy; but whether the monarch in question was Josiah (Alt), Hezekiah (Kallai-Kleinmann), Uzziah (Aharoni), Jehoshaphat (Cross and Wright) or some other appears to be still an open question.[42] In the Judahite list Kiriath-baal (Kiriath-jearim) and Rabbah form a unit by themselves. Rabbah is probably to be identified with *r u b u t e* of the cuneiform inscriptions and *r b t* of

Egyptian topographical lists, and if Aharoni is right in identifying both with Beth-shemesh we would have an interesting confirmation of the relation between the two cities in the ark-narrative in I Sam. vi. 10 – vii. 1.[43] We may take it that it was originally in Benjamin, as were the other cities listed with it in Joshua xviii. 21–8, and that it later formed part of a separate province of the Kingdom of Judah associated closely with Jerusalem.[44]

Mazar and Aharoni claim to find Kiriath-jearim in the account of Sheshonk's Asiatic campaign referred to earlier, but the *q d t m* of this text seems to be situated between Aijalon and Beth-horon which does not easily fit the site of Kiriath-jearim.[45] There can be little doubt that this city lay in the neighbourhood of Karyet el-'Enab about fourteen miles west of Jerusalem on the old Jaffa road, more precisely, Tell el-'Azhar alongside the road.[46] It does not occur in the Amarna letters nor in any other non-biblical text known to us.

Kiriath-jearim is the only Gibeonite city attributed to Judah in the lists and the only one which plays a part in the Jerusalemite narratives about the ark in I Sam.[47] In a later chapter we shall endeavour to throw some light on both the significance of the Gibeonite enclave as a whole and the religious history of Israel in the pre-monarchical and early-monarchical period by examining more closely this early Jerusalemite ark-tradition. In attempting this task we shall have to take account not just of the relevant texts in the early historical narratives but of other references to the city which are highly problematic. These must include the topographical 'genealogy' of the Chronicler in which Kiriath-jearim is related collaterally to Bethlehem, both descended from Ephrathah (I Chron. ii. 50*b*), and 'the fields of Jaar', parallel with Ephrathah, in which the ark was discovered (Ps. cxxxii. 6). The absence of any reference to the ark from the time when the inhabitants of Kiriath-jearim took it from the Beth-shemeshites to the time when David brought it to Jerusalem[48] creates a special problem for anyone attempting this task but also makes it more urgent to examine all the evidence, whether direct or indirect, which is available.

The order in which the Gibeonite cities are listed in Joshua ix.17 does not seem to have any special significance apart from indicating that Gibeon was, in a sense, the metropolis. Hertzberg suggested an east-to-west order but this is not possible with the identifications proposed above.[49]

Since the identification of Benjaminite Mizpah has been inseparably linked with that of the Gibeonite cities a word must be said on this subject before going any further. The forms Mizpeh and Mizpah seem to be interchangeable, to judge by Joshua xi.3, 8 (the 'land of Mizpah' inhabited by Hivites and the 'valley of Mizpeh'). Mizpeh is one of fourteen cities in the second half of the Benjaminite city-list (Joshua xviii.26); elsewhere the name of the Benjaminite city is always Mizpah. That the place-name, wherever it occurs, always has the article (with the sole exception of Hos. v.1) is of course to be explained by the meaning of the word itself ('watch-tower', 'lookout-post'). Benjaminite Mizpah is the site of an important sanctuary in the story of the crime of Gibeah and the military action taken by the tribes against Benjamin as a result of it (Judges xx–xxi), and it was at Mizpah that Samuel convoked the tribal assembly described in 1 Sam. vii.5ff. and designated Saul as king (1 Sam. x.17ff.). In the war between Baasha and the Judahite–Syrian allies the former was unable to proceed with his plan for fortifying Ramah and material from the site was used by Asa to build up the defences of Geba and Mizpah (1 Kings xv.22). The same city assumed great importance in the exilic period after it was chosen as the administrative centre of the diminished Kingdom of Judah (2 Kings xxv.22ff. and Jer. lx–lxi). A Mizpah opposite Jerusalem was the scene of penitential rites carried out by Judas during the Maccabean age on the grounds that 'there was in former days a place of prayer at Mizpah for Israel' (1 Macc. iii.46).

We need not rehearse in detail the arguments adduced in the modern period in support of an identification with either Tell en-Naṣbeh or Nebi Samwil.[50] In view of the name itself, designating a common topographical feature, it seems surprising that so few have contemplated the possibility that both places could have borne this name. We would suggest that the sanctuary referred to in Judges and 1 Sam. is Nebi Samwil which was also, in all probability, the central sanctuary of the Gibeonite cities. It may not therefore be entirely coincidental that both the Gibeonite area and the 'land of Mizpah' in the Beqa (Joshua xi.3) were inhabited by Hivites. Moreover, Gibeon and Mizpah are closely associated in the narrative of events following on the assassination of Gedaliah (Jer. xli.4ff.) and 'the men of Gibeon and of Mizpah' worked together in repairing the walls of Jerusalem after the return from exile (Neh. iii.7). It has often been noted that in Judges and 1 Sam. Mizpah occurs in a late strand of the literary tradition.[51] Certain similarities in style and religious outlook between this strand and the prose passages in Jeremiah and the Deuteronomist history reinforce this view and help to explain the references to Mizpah in the early history.[52] Nebi Samwil may therefore have been known in the earlier period as *ha-Giḇʿāh*, later as *ha-Miṣpāh*.

We have, finally, no means of knowing the location of the ha-Mizpeh of the Benjaminite city-list (Joshua xviii.26).

## CHAPTER II

# THE ETHNIC IDENTITY OF THE GIBEONITES

In Joshua ix.7 and xi.19 the Gibeonites are described as Hivites (*ḥiwwî*) and in 2 Sam. xxi.2 as non-Israelite, 'part of the residue of the Amorites'. In the present chapter we shall see whether it is possible to establish the meaning of these terms in the context of biblical usage and of whatever evidence is available from other sources.

The Old Testament contains some twenty-one lists, of a more or less stereotype nature, of ethnic groups in Canaan at the time of the Israelite settlement.[1] The Hivites occur in eighteen of these, generally (fourteen times) second-last, followed by the Jebusites. They are distinct from Amorites and Hittites since these also occur in the lists. Num. xxii.29 (LXX) places Hivites in the hill country together with Hittites, Jebusites and Amorites while Joshua xi.3 (LXX) has Amorites, Hivites, Jebusites and Perizzites dwelling in that region. In view of the close historical association between Gibeon and Jerusalem the fact that Hivites and Jebusites occur so frequently together may well be significant. LXX Εὐαῖοι translates *ḥiwwî* though there is occasional confusion between 'Hivite', 'Hittite' and 'Horite'.[2]

Apart from the lists, the biblical evidence locates Hivites in three fairly well defined areas. Gen. xxxiv.2 speaks of Shechem ben-Hamor the Hivite though here, as in Joshua ix.7, LXX[B] has Χορραῖος which presupposes *ḥōrî* identical with *ḥurrî* (tone-long *o* before *resh*).[3] Judges iii.3 numbers among the nations left to test the Israelites 'the Hivites who dwelt on Mount Lebanon from Mount Baal-Hermon as far as the Entrance of Hamath'. According to Joshua xi.3 there are Hivites in 'the land of Mizpah' (cf. verse 8, 'the valley of Mizpeh') under Hermon, and in the narrative of David's census-commission we read that his officials came 'to the fortress of Tyre and to all the cities of the Hivites and Canaanites' (2 Sam. xxiv.7). This clearly refers to the same region. We have just seen that, according to LXX, Hivites were established together with other groups in the central hill country which would accord with the description of the Gibeonites as a Hivite group, especially in view of the close associations between Gibeon and Jerusalem. Finally, Gen. xxxvi.29 refers to Zibeon, son of Seir the Horite, himself a Horite chieftain. In verse 2 the same person is described as a Hivite.

This last raises at once the vexed question of the relation between Hivite and Horite in the Old Testament and in history. Since the time of Eduard Meyer it has generally been assumed that the biblical Horites are identical with the Hurrians of the cuneiform and hieroglyphic inscriptions.[4] *Ḥōrî* is identical with *ḥurrî* (cf. Eg. *ḥuru*, Ug. *ḫry* and Acc. *ḫurri*), Palestine is known as *ḥuru* (*ḥr*) in Egyptian inscriptions from about the middle of the sixteenth century, and the same term appears in connection with Canaan and Israel on the Merneptah stele.[5] The archaeological evidence points to a steadily increasing hurrianization in Syria beginning in the eighteenth century. The Alalakh (Tell el-'Aṭshānah) tablets from level VII (ca. 1700 B.C.) contain only a few Hurrian names but those from level IV, between two and three centuries later, show a very high degree of Hurrian presence and influence, with the city itself owing allegiance to the king of Mitanni.[6] Texts wholly in Hurrian have been discovered at Ugarit (Ras Shamra) and the administrative texts give some idea of the extent of Hurrian presence in northern Syria in the fifteenth century.[7] By the same time both Aleppo and Qatna had become predominantly Hurrian,[8] and it may be recalled that the biblical texts place Hivites not so far south of Qatna in the Beqa. That the Hurrian movement westward and southward did not stop in Syria is established by archaeological evidence from Megiddo, Taanach and Shechem,[9] and by the time of the Amarna letters there can be no doubt that Hurrians had penetrated deeply and in considerable numbers into Palestine.[10]

In view of the evidence for this widespread Hurrian movement to the west and south it was natural to presume some connection between these Hurrian groups and the Hyksos who achieved political dominance in Egypt and Palestine from the beginning of the seventeenth century to shortly before the middle of the sixteenth century. Since, however, the great majority of Hyksos names known to us are clearly Semitic,[11] it would be hazardous to make too much of this, though we need not go to the other extreme and deny *any* association between Hyksos and Hurrians.

In order to have reliable criteria for establishing the existence and extent of Hurrian presence in any given region we have to depend on onomastics, reference in the texts to *maryannu*, the chariot-aristocracy of Mitanni and their characteristic equipment and, less clearly, certain artistic and architectural features.[12] By applying only those criteria which he considers relevant, de Vaux has arrived at the conclusion that the Hurrians entered Palestine in the first quarter of the fifteenth century, that although they obtained political control in the principal cities they never went beyond a small minority of the population, and that after the Amarna period they were quickly assimilated into the indigenous culture.[13] From the well known biblical references to Horites and Hivites he concludes that in neither case has the Old Testament preserved any genuine memory of the Hurrians. The Horites are not identical with the Hurrians since the biblical evidence places them in a region (Edom) where we have no reason to believe Hurrians ever settled. Reference to pre-Edomite Horites in Seir (Gen. xiv.6; Deut. ii.12, 22; Gen. xxxvi) is to be explained by the fact that the Israelites arbitrarily limited the appellation *ḫuru* to the Transjordanian region, reserving 'Canaan' for Palestine proper. While it is true that the biblical texts place Hivites in regions where we know Hurrians settled, by the time of the Israelite occupation these Hurrians of the Amarna period were assimilated to the local population. We do not know who the Hivites were but at least they were not Hurrians.

This thesis of de Vaux, which contradicts not only widely

held views about the biblical Horites but also his own previously held opinions,[14] raises some serious questions. In the first place, the natural assumption would be that the Hurrians did not within the space of little more than a century disappear from the Palestinian scene after the break-up of the Mitanni empire towards the end of the Amarna period (ca. 1360 B.C.). It is important to note that, particularly after this date, Hurrians are not necessarily associated with Indo-aryans. Once the political power of this Hurrian state had been destroyed we no longer need validate Hurrian presence by reference to a particular type of urban culture or military and social organization. Failure to take account of this seriously weakens the arguments produced by de Vaux and others to exclude the possibility of Hurrian settlements in Edom.[15] Moreover, it is difficult to imagine why the Israelites would have arbitrarily limited *ḥuru* to Edom. Biblical references to ethnic groups in pre-Israelite Canaan and the surrounding area are not limited to generalities but often indicate with a fair degree of precision the location of non-Israelite ethnic groups. While we may admit the general validity of de Vaux's explanation of the terms Canaanite, Amorite and Hittite as reflecting different redactional strata, its limitations in practice can be shown, for example, by the fact that both Gibeonites and the anti-Gibeonite allies are referred to as Amorites (Joshua x.5; 2 Sam. xxi.2) though only the former are described as Hivites.

The impossibility of locating Hurrians in Edom is deduced from the lack of any archaeological evidence and the names of Horite clans in Gen. xxxvi, all of which are Semitic. As to the former, we may ask whether too much is not expected of the surface explorations of Nelson Glueck in Transjordan.[16] If the pre-Edomite Horites–Hurrians of Gen. xxxvi had taken to a nomadic or semi-nomadic existence after the collapse of the Mitanni empire, a possibility which Glueck himself leaves open, we would hardly have expected the kind of archaeological data which has emerged from sites further north.[17] This whole question is also complicated by our uncertainty as to the extent of early Edom. All the biblical texts which locate

Horites in Edom mention Seir which lies to the south of the Negeb and west of Wadi el-'Arabah. According to Num. xxxiv.3 Edom is to the south of Israel and in Joshua xv.1 it lies along the southern boundary of Judah. Early historical tradition is conscious of close association between Edomites or pre-Edomites, Kenites and Kenizzites, and these last two settled in the Negeb, some of them as far north as Hebron.[18] We may add that of all the ethnic terms found in these early traditions *Kenizzi* comes closest to a Hurrian form, and it has long been suspected that the names of the Anakim settled from early times around Hebron may well be Hurrian.[19]

While it would be rash simply to equate Hivites with Horites–Hurrians, with or without the help of arbitrary textual emendation, it would seem reasonable to suppose some connection between them even if the nature of this association cannot be precisely defined. In Gen. xxxvi Zibeon is described as both Hivite (verse 2) and Horite (verse 29, cf. verse 20), and it would be premature to emend 'Hivite' in verse 2 to 'Horite', especially in view of the correspondence between some of the names in this chapter and others belonging to the Hivites of the Gibeonite cities.[20] Nor should we neglect the clear witness of early biblical tradition to a close *ethnic* association between Israel and Edom at the very beginning of the history of these peoples, as well as the existence of groups whose association with both Israelite and Edomite clans was close.[21] Finally, we have seen that the Cisjordan Hivites are located precisely in those regions where the inscriptions would lead us to expect Hurrian presence.

We have at present no means of explaining the derivation of *ḥiwwî*. Albright suggests comparison with *ḥ a w w ô ṯ* (as in Num. xxxii.4) and Arabic *ḥ i w a ' u n* (=a group of tents) or possibly the early tribal name *ḥ w y*.[22] In his treatment of Gen. xxxvi he proposes the drastic expedient of eliminating *ḥōrî* completely since there is no evidence of Hurrian penetration into Edom. The Hivites are to be located here and here only, and therefore he logically rejects M.T. *ḥiwwî* Gen. xxxiv.2 and Joshua ix.7 in favour of LXX.[23] The closest analogies to the personal and tribal names in Gen. xxxvi are not Hurrian but Arabic, following the careful study of B. Moritz.[24]

This explanation of Albright is unacceptable if for no other reason than that it completely reverses the evidence of M.T. in which all the occurrences of *ḥōrî* refer to Edom. It also suffers from too great a reliance on the results of Glueck's surface exploration as constituting an adequate *argumentum e silentio*. In addition, certain reservations could be voiced with respect to the Arabic parallels adduced by Moritz, without however accepting the premature attempts of Feiler, Ginsberg, Maisler (Mazar) and others to trace most of these names to a Hurrian origin.[25] The Arabic comparative material comes for the most part from a late date, in some cases from the immediate pre-Islamic period, but in any case from long after the Hurrian element would have been absorbed.[26] And it would not be out of place to note that *some* of the names in this chapter are equally susceptible of a Hurrian as they are of an Arabic derivation, though the conclusions in both cases will be hypothetical.[27]

E. A. Speiser, one of the most eminent scholars in the field of Hurrian studies, was also impressed by the lack of any evidence for Hurrian presence in pre-monarchical Edom but suggested a solution different from that of Albright. 'Horite' and 'Hivite' are virtually synonymous, as the example of Zibeon shows, but these Edomite Horites are quite different ethnically from those on the other side of the Jordan. The former are Semitic (probably 'cave-dwellers'), the latter genuinely Hurrian.[28] 'Hivite' is explained simply as 'one of the terms that MT applies to the Hurrians'[29] and no derivation is put forward apart from a suggested comparison with a Hyksos group named *ʿ a w w i m*.[30] It may be noted that the Avvim mentioned in Deut. ii.23 and Joshua xiii are translated in LXX by Εὐαῖοι which also serves for Hivites (Hebrew *ʿ w y* cf. *ḥ w y*), though we have no means of establishing any further relation between the two groups.[31]

Recently G. E. Mendenhall has proposed that the Hivites

originated in the region of Asia Minor corresponding to the kingdom of Kizzuwadna which came into the Hittite sphere of influence during the reign of Suppiluliumas (1380–1340 B.C.).[32] This hypothesis implies that *ḥ w y* derives from *q u w e*, the inhabitants of the region referred to in Assyrian inscriptions from the mid-ninth century as *q u e* (*q a w e*).[33] A final evaluation of Mendenhall's suggestion is impossible at this stage because of the paucity of the material. If accepted, it would not by any means exclude Hurrian affinities with Hivites since Hurrian presence is strongly attested both in Kizzuwadna and in northern Syria.

Another and older hypothesis which has been advanced to explain the presence of an ethnically mixed population in the central highlands of Palestine, and which therefore would be relevant to the question of Hivite origins, is that of E. O. Forrer with respect to the so-called Pestilence Prayer of Mursilis II (ca. 1339–1306 B.C.).[34] This text refers to a plague which had been raging in the land of Hatti since the time of Suppiluliumas. An oracle had drawn the king's attention to two tablets which were held to contain the explanation of the outbreak, and one of these concerned a city in northern Anatolia called Kurustamma the inhabitants of which had been transferred by the Hittites (or perhaps had emigrated) to 'the land of Egypt'. These were the subject of a treaty made with the Egyptians under the auspices of Teshub the Hittite (originally Hurrian) storm-god. The Hittites had violated this treaty in invading 'the land of Amka' which must also have been considered part of 'the land of Egypt'.[35] The expedition was successful, but the prisoners brought back from the campaign were responsible for the outbreak of the epidemic. Forrer suggested that this settlement of an Anatolian group in territory under Egyptian suzerainty might explain the references to 'Hittite' elements in the central highlands of Palestine.

Unfortunately we know neither the ethnic identity of the 'people of Kurustamma' nor where exactly in 'the land of Egypt' they settled. Since we may suppose some connection between their movement from the land of Hatti and the invasion of 'the land of Amka' we would be inclined to think of this as their new abode; in which case the biblical references to Hivites in the same region (Joshua xi.3, 8; Judges iii.3) would be particularly significant. We may also find some striking similarities between the treaty referred to in this text and that between Israelites and the Hivites of Gibeon. In both cases the violation of the treaty leads to a public calamity in the following reign (2 Sam. xxi.1ff.). Both Mursilis and David seek enlightenment from an oracle on the cause of the calamity and are referred back to a previous treaty violation; and the conformity of the Gibeonites' demand (2 Sam. xxi.5f.) with the retribution clause in Hittite treaties makes the parallelism even more striking.[36] If we may suppose some connection between Hivites in the Beqa and in the region north-west of Jerusalem[37] this text would provide a plausible explanation both of the origin of this non-Israelite group and the absence of any reference to it in the Amarna letters and earlier documents.[38] In this case the Gibeonites may, after all, have arrived from a far country not very long before the Israelite settlement.

We may refer, finally, to the conjecture of B. Hrozný, taken up by J. Heller, which connects *ḥiwwî* with *Ḥawwāh* of Gen. iii.20 understood as a transcription of the name of the great Hurrian goddess Ḫepat.[39]

The conclusions which we draw from this investigation may be summarized as follows. 'Hivite' is not identical with 'Horite' and must not be made so by arbitrary textual emendation. A relationship does, however, exist between Hivites and Horites (Hurrians) though its precise nature cannot be established at present. It seems more probable that the Hivites represented a separate group having affinities with the Hurrians rather than a term synonymous with them or one of several subdivisions. None of the hypotheses so far advanced to explain the origins of the Palestinian Hivites goes beyond a probability, and some of them are not even probable.

We now turn briefly to the description of the Gibeonites in

2 Sam. xxi.2 as 'of the remnant of the Amorites' (*miyyeṯer ha'ᵉmōrî*). This occurs in what appears to be an explanatory gloss which stresses that the Gibeonites were ethnically non-Israelite. It may be considered parallel with the Elohist's use of the term 'Amorite' (cf. 'Canaanite' in J) to designate the pre-Israelite and non-Israelite population of Canaan in the most general way.[40] The Gibeonites are, at any rate, clearly differentiated from the 'Amorites' who leagued against them and were defeated in the famous battle (see Joshua ix.7; xi.17); and the difference may be further confirmed by the absence of any reference to a king in the making of the treaty. Gibeon is not the only region where we know non-Israelite and non-Semitic populations settled and yet which are described in the Old Testament as 'Amorite'. Shechem, eponymous founder of the city, is Hivite (Gen. xxxiv.2) and yet Jacob affirms that he captured the city from the Amorites (Gen. xlviii.22).[41] Mamre is Amorite (Gen. xiv.13) yet 'the people of the land' are Hittite (Gen. xxiii.3ff.; xlix.29f.; l.13). In both cases there is non-biblical evidence for non-Semitic elements in the local populations in an earlier period.[42]

We have no lack of evidence for an ethnically mixed population in the Central Highlands, especially in and around Jerusalem, at the time of the Israelite settlement. The spies' report (Num. xiii.29) speaks of Hittites, Jebusites and Amorites in the hill country. Ezekiel's allegory on Jerusalem, whose father was an Amorite and mother a Hittite, points in the same direction (xvi.45). Though we have few positive indications as to the exact connotation of either 'Hittite' or 'Jebusite' in this context, it has long been suspected that both may imply a Hurrian element.[43]

In the early document on the settlement contained in Judges i the Amorites settle in what will later be the tribal territory of Dan and control a good part of that region (verses 34–6). After driving the Danites back into the hill country, in the direction of Benjamin, they themselves are defeated by the Joseph tribes and put to forced labour. This is parallel to the fate of the Gibeonite 'Amorites' in Benjaminite territory since they too preserved their independence for some time before being reduced to servitude as 'hewers of wood and drawers of water' (Joshua ix. 21, 23, 27). The content of 1 Sam. vii. 2ff. would lead us to suppose that the 'Amorites' with whom there was peace during the judgeship of Samuel were, or at least included, the Gibeonites. In a later chapter we shall pursue further the question of non-Israelite elements and religious practices in the neighbouring tribes of Dan and Benjamin.[44]

The main criterion to be applied, if with caution, in attempting to determine the ethnic composition of a population in a particular area is the incidence of personal names. On this basis it has been established, for example, that a symbiosis or at least juxtaposition of Semitic and Hurrian existed at Nuzi around 1500 B.C. and in several Syrian and Palestinian cities during the second half of the same millennium.[45] In the case of the Gibeonite cities we have, apart from the personal names preserved in the Old Testament, only those which have come to light at el-Jîb. These names cannot be dated earlier than the seventh century and several of them occur in the Old Testament from the time of Jeremiah or shortly after – including that of the Gibeonite prophet Hananiah, opponent of Jeremiah.[46] It will be of interest to note that at least five of the el-Jîb personal names are found in post-exilic lists of minor cultic personnel attached to the Jerusalem temple, a fact which may well be significant in view of the connection between the Gibeonites and the *nethinim* of that period.[47] Apart from this, the names are too late to be relevant in any way to the early history of the city and the question of the ethnic identity of its inhabitants. The same must be said of other Gibeonite personal names in the Old Testament: Melatiah (Neh. iii.7), Ishmaiah (1 Chron. xii.4) and Uriah ben-Shemaiah of Kiriath-jearim (Jer. xxvi.20).[48]

Apart from Abinadab and Eleazar of Kiriath-jearim (1 Sam. vii.1), whose names will be discussed in a later chapter, the only other personal names of inhabitants of the Gibeonite cities occurring in early texts are Baanah and Rechab, sons of the Beerothite Rimmon (2 Sam. iv.2), and Naharai of Beeroth, armour-bearer of Joab (2 Sam. xxiii.37). It has been suggested that Baanah derives from Ben-Anah,[49] which would be interesting in view of the occurrence of Anah in an Edomite list (Gen. xxxvi.2) and the suggested Hurrian derivation for this name.[50] In 2 Sam. xxiii.29 a warrior of David bears this name (Baanah). His city is Netophah which is mentioned in 1 Chron. ii.54 as related to clans settled near Kiriath-jearim. The Baanah of 1 Kings iv.12 is in charge of the district which includes Taanach and Megiddo both of which had a Hurrian element in the pre-Israelite period. Another Baanah is in charge of the district of Asher and Bealoth (iv.16); his father is Hushai (cf. Husham, Gen. xxxvi.34). Rechab can hardly be dissociated from the Rechabites, closely related to the Kenites according to the 'genealogical' system of the Chronicler (1 Chron. ii.55). Both are probably derived from the north-west Semitic storm-deity *r k b* attested in early Aramaic inscriptions. Rimmon bears the name of a deity worshipped in Syria, Assyria, the neighbourhood of Megiddo and probably also the Negeb. This deity was identified with the storm-god Hadad, as is clear from Zech. xii.11 and the name of Tab-rimmon's son, Ben-hadad in 1 Kings xv.18;[51] also with Teshub, the great storm-god of the Hurrians.[52] We may note that Hadad occurs as a personal name of a *ḫabiru* in the hurrianized city of Nuzi and is borne by at least one of the early Edomite kings.[53] In view of the frequent representation of Yahweh as a storm-god it is not without interest to note that Teshub, standing on a bull and holding the *lituus*, or being drawn in a chariot through the sky, is well attested in Hurrian iconography.[54] In this guise he corresponds to Hadad (Baal) described in the Ugaritic texts as *r k b ʿ r p t* (cf. Ps. lxviii.4).[55]

Further lists of names, mostly of clans, are to be found in the first part of the Chronicler's work (1 Chron. ii.50*b*–55 concerning Kiriath-jearim, viii.29–32 and ix.35–8 concerning Gibeon). As is now generally recognized, these lists contain much genuinely pre-exilic material though arranged according to the specific intentions of the Chronicler.[56] The list in which the 'family' of Kiriath-jearim occurs is probably Calebite rather than Hezronite,[57] and we may recall that the Calebites were closely related to the Kenizzites whose territory was in the Negeb and southwards, who almost certainly contained a Hurrian element and who also had racial affinities with some early settlers of Edom.[58] Significantly, Manahathites (1 Chron. ii.54) are associated with Kiriath-jearim in some way and are also found in early Edom (Gen. xxxvi.23). In both cases the *heros eponymos* is Shobal, a name for which a Hurrian origin has been suggested.[59] We may also compare Hur, 'father' of Shobal (1 Chron. ii.50*b*), with the Hori of the Edomite lists who was descended from Seir the Horite (Gen. xxxvi.22).[60]

The genealogy goes on to list clans settled at some time in the neighbourhood of Kiriath-jearim: Ithrites, Puthites, Shumathites and Mishraites, from which the inhabitants of the Danite cities of Zorah and Eshtaol were in some way descended. The gentilic Ithri is practically identical with the clan-name Ithran in the Edomite lists (Gen. xxxvi.26) and with Jethro the Midianite (Kenite) father of Moses' wife (Exod. iii.1, etc.). Among the Thirty, David's *corps d'élite*, are numbered two Ithrites, Ira and Gareb, whose names occur between Naharai of Beeroth and Uriah the Hittite (2 Sam. xxiii.38 = 1 Chron. xi.40). This may indicate that the warriors in this part of the list were of Gibeonite origin. The gentilic Puthi is a *hapax legomenon.* In the absence of any satisfactory Semitic derivation of this name we may suggest Hurrian *puti* (servant [of a god]) as in puti-ḫeba (Abdi-Ḫepat) king of Jerusalem in the Amarna letters.[61] Shumathi and Mishrai are also *hapax legomena* and of unknown derivation.

Turning to the two parallel versions of the Gibeonite 'genealogy', we find the most surprising aspect of these lists to be the inclusion of the family of Saul. In a later chapter we shall try to explain why Saul, who carried out hostile activity against the Gibeonites, should be found in a Gibeonite genealogy. To speak of various 'sons' (cities or ethnic groups) born of a 'marriage' between Jeiel father of Gibeon and Maacah is for the Chronicler a way of representing either the results of racial symbiosis or the resettling of groups in a different locality; in which case it may be significant that the name Maacah also features in a Calebite genealogy (1 Chron. ii.48). There follow the names of ten descendants of the Gibeonite forefather. It is difficult to tell from verse 32*b* whether they are represented as dwelling in Gibeon 'opposite their kinsmen in Jerusalem' or in Jerusalem itself. If the latter, they may well reflect the tradition associating Gibeonites with the post-exilic *nethinim*. As is clear from 1 Chron. viii.23, Abdon, the first of the list, is a Benjaminite name. The same name occurs in 2 Chron. xxxiv.20 but the parallel 2 Kings xxii.12 reads Achbor, a name which occurs in the Edomite king-list (Gen. xxxvi.38). The name Zur is also borne by a Midianite (Num. xxv.15, etc.). Kish, Baal and Ner provide the link with the Saulite list and will be discussed in a later chapter. Nadab is a name intimately associated with the Levitical cult service, reminding us that Gibeon was a Levitical city.[62] Gedor may be compared with the Geder of the Hur list (iv.4) and the place-name occurring frequently among the el-Jîb graffiti.[63] Ahio is also a Benjaminite name (cf. viii.14) and we recall that Uzzah and Ahio were the bearers of the ark from its sojourn among the Gibeonites to Jerusalem (2 Sam. vi.3, 4). It may be noted that personal names formed with *'aḥ-*, *'aḥi-* are met with frequently among Gibeonites, Saulites and cultic personnel associated with the ark.[64] Zecher is practically identical with Zichri commonly found among both Benjaminites and Levites.[65] Mikloth is found only here and in 1 Chron. xxvii.4 belonging to an officer of David. With Shimeah (cf. ix.38 Shimeam) we may compare the Edomite name Shammah (Gen. xxxvi.13), though the latter does not have the *aleph*.

The purpose of this brief survey of Gibeonite personal names is not to prove that the Gibeonites were Hurrian or at least non-Semitic – it is evidently incapable of doing that. What it does show, however, is an interesting overlap with names in Edom and in the region south of Judah. In doing this it confirms indirectly the biblical evidence for non-Semitic, and, in particular, Hivite elements in both Canaan and Edom and supports our contention of some association between Hivites and the

Hurrians of the inscriptions. This indirect evidence is in its turn supported by some topographical names associated with the Gibeonite cities. Baalah, identified with Kiriath-jearim in Joshua xv. 9, also occurs as a city name 'in the extreme South, towards the boundary of Edom' (xv. 29) as does Chesil (cf. Chesalon, another name for Mount Jearim, xv. 10). In the same boundary description, moreover, Mount Seir occurs next to Mount Jearim. The name Jearim itself can hardly be dissociated from 'the fields of Jaar' in which the ark was found (Ps. cxxxii. 6), and in this text 'the fields of Jaar' is in parallelism with Ephrathah, a name which stands at the head of the Chronicler's genealogy to which Kiriath-jearim belongs (1 Chron. ii. 50*b*). Ephrathah is often identified with Bethlehem in the Old Testament though, as we shall see, it was originally in Benjamin; and we have, finally, the much discussed and textually corrupt reference to Jaar the Bethlehemite whose son slew Goliath according to 2 Sam. xxi. 19. These indications, confused as they are, point to an important aspect of the Gibeonite question which has been widely neglected and which we shall examine more carefully at a further point in this study.

## CHAPTER III

# THE GIBEONITE–ISRAELITE TREATY

We may take it as certain that the Gibeonites constituted an enclave which was ethnically distinct from other elements described as 'Amorite' (Joshua x.5) and, *a fortiori*, from the Israelites. After the death of Saul they are still 'not of the people of Israel' (2 Sam. xxi.2) and as late as the reign of Solomon the Gibeonite sanctuary can be described as 'the great high place' (1 Kings iii.4). It was only with Solomon's administrative reorganization of the kingdom (1 Kings iv.7–19) and his subjection of ethnic minorities to forced labour (ix.20–1)[1] that the Gibeonites lost their distinctive character.

We saw earlier that the main difficulty in reconstructing the early history of Gibeon is its absence from any inscription of the second millennium and the fact that the excavations at el-Jîb have revealed no significant evidence for a Late Bronze settlement.[2] In view of the fact that at one stage of the Israelite settlement it is described as 'a great city, like one of the royal cities' (Joshua x.2) and was obviously a force to be reckoned with from the military point of view (x.2*b*), this silence might seem to call for an explanation.[3] Particularly significant is the absence of any mention of Gibeon in the Amarna letters, which testify so strongly to the importance of Jerusalem to the south and Shechem to the north. How is this to be explained?

One possibility, already alluded to, is that during the Amarna period Gibeon lay within the *mâtu* (land) of Jerusalem. el-Jîb is no more than eight miles from the temple area and the biblical record provides evidence of fairly close cultural relations between the two cities. Both had a mixed population: the Gibeonites are described as Hivites and Amorites, Jerusalem was at the head of an Amorite alliance against Gibeon (Joshua x.1, 5) and the pre-Israelite city was inhabited by Jebusites. Hivites and Jebusites occur together in thirteen of the stereotype lists of pre-Israelite populations (second-last and last). We know nothing directly about the ethnic character of the Jebusites but the Hurrian name of the Amarna king, who was born in Jerusalem,[4] and possibly also the name Araunah, suggest Hurrian affinities. The anti-Jerusalemite allegory of Ezekiel seems to trace apostasy from Yahweh to ethnic intermarriage (xvi.3, 45) and we have seen that in this context 'Hittite' is an ethnic rather than a political term. A similar situation must have obtained around Hebron since in Gen. xxiii.7 and elsewhere the 'people of the land' are described as Hittites. Hebron is not named in the Amarna letters but a king living in or near Hebron has an Indo-aryan name, Šuwardata,[5] and the Anakim names in Num. xiii.22 and Judges i.10 are not Semitic. In the early stages of the settlement of the South Hebron is given to a Kenizzite clan which, as we have seen, almost certainly had Hurrian affinities.

Indirect confirmation of association between the Gibeonite cities and Jerusalem of the Amarna period may be found in some widely overlooked though significant evidence in the Old Testament for ethnic affinity between Kiriath-jearim and Bethlehem.[6] The latter occurs in the Amarna letters as a 'city of the land of Jerusalem', and the same may have been the case with the Gibeonite cities.[7] This hypothesis would be consonant with the hostile reaction of Adonizedek to the treaty (Joshua x.1ff.) since the alliance of Gibeonites with Israelites would then have constituted a renunciation of allegiance of the kind frequently evidenced in the letters. That Amarna Jerusalem touched on Gezer to the north and very probably also included Beth-shemesh within its boundaries[8] increases the probability that the Gibeonite region lay within the jurisdiction of the king of Jerusalem.

One merit of this hypothesis is that it fits well with evidence direct or indirect in the biblical tradition for close political and religious ties between the two cities. David brought the ark to Jerusalem from a Gibeonite city (2 Sam. vi.1ff.) and Solomon, though already established in Jerusalem, continued to frequent the Gibeonite sanctuary (1 Kings iii.4). For the Chronicler Gibeon plays a very important role in the early cultic history of Israel since it was there that the Mosaic Tent and the altar made by Bezalel were located (1 Chron. xvi.39; 2 Chron. i.5; xxi.29). Even more surprisingly, he associates the priest Zadok very closely with Gibeon (1 Chron. xvi.37ff.) raising the question, for some scholars, whether Zadok may not have been of Gibeonite rather than Jerusalemite origin.[9] We may add that the *Lives of the Prophets* states that Nathan came from Gibeon and was buried there,[10] a piece of information which we have no means of substantiating or, for that matter, of denying.

But even if Gibeon was part of 'the land of Jerusalem' in the first half of the fourteenth century the absence of any mention of it in the letters would nevertheless lead us to suppose, with Albright,[11] that it was of no particular importance at that time and we should therefore be led to enquire – presuming the correct assessment of its importance in Joshua x.2 – how it came to assume such importance. At this point we are, quite clearly, in the realm of hypothesis. We know too little of the history of Palestine between the end of the Amarna period and the main thrust of the Israelite settlement, generally dated in the second half of the thirteenth century,[12] to make any confident pronouncement. It may be suggested that the establishment of a strong Hivite enclave north-west of Jerusalem is connected in some way with the break-up of the Mitanni empire towards the end of the Amarna period or the settlement of a group originating in Anatolia or Syria. The translocation of the people of Kurustamma has already been discussed in this respect, and no doubt this was not an isolated case.[13] This, we repeat, is no more than a hypothesis the degree of probability of which has to be measured against other factors involved some of which will be alluded to in this chapter.

At the time of the treaty the Gibeonite cities formed an identifiable political unity. Not only do they act as a body in making the treaty – whether or not the *'ereṣ* of Joshua ix.11 refers to their present location – but the demand for retribution in 2 Sam. xxi.4ff. is made by the Gibeonites as a whole since not just the city of Gibeon alone was affected.[14] In this respect the 'land of Mizpah' in the Beqa (Joshua xi.3) provides, as we have seen, an interesting parallel. In this context *'ereṣ* would probably have much the same meaning as *mâtu* in the Amarna letters – a metropolis surrounded by dependent cities. The narrative of the execution of the Saulites makes it probable, moreover, that the Gibeonites worshipped at a central sanctuary (2 Sam. xxi.6, 9), probably to be identified with Nebi Samwil.[15] It would seem that, in some important respects, the term 'amphictyony' would apply more exactly to this kind of organization, similar to the Philistine cities, than it does to the Israelite tribes.

It may be added that what little we know of conditions in Palestine in the decades following the Amarna period provides some support for this interpretation of the biblical tradition on the Gibeonite cities. There seems to have been a tendency at that time for larger political units to emerge incorporating the smaller city-states, and this tendency was particularly in evidence along the Central Highlands.[16]

The description of Gibeon as 'like one of the royal cities' (Joshua x.2) suggests that it was not ruled by a king as were the Amorite cities leagued against it. The 'elders' (ix.11) play the leading role in making the treaty and there is no mention of a king, which we might legitimately have expected if Gibeon had been a monarchy. We know that oligarchic rule of cities did exist alongside the monarchic city-states before the Amarna period in Palestine,[17] and this may well have continued indefinitely thereafter. In Gen. xxxiv Hamor the Hivite prince of the 'land' (verse 2) of Shechem negotiated the treaty with 'the sons of Jacob' but was obliged to have it ratified by the assembly of free citizens (verses 20–4). The Abimelech episode at Ophrah and Shechem (Judges ix) is probably to be interpreted as an attempt to impose a hereditary kingship on people accustomed to a kind of oligarchic rule similar to that obtaining in predominantly Hurrian centres.[18] At a later stage we shall suggest that this may help to explain the mutual hostility which arose between Saul and the Gibeonites.

The political situation presupposed by Joshua ix–x. 1–5 fits in almost disconcertingly well with what we know of political conditions in Palestine during the Amarna age. The letters reveal the rapid formation and equally rapid disintegration of coalitions. Jerusalem and the 'land' to the south (around Hebron or Keilah) ally against the *'apiru* but we also find Jerusalem facing an alliance of her former ally with Gezer. The alliance between Labaya of Shechem and the *'apiru* is not so different from that between Gibeonites and Israelites. In fact, if we had not good reason to date the historical substratum of Joshua ix–x later than the Amarna age,[19] we could hardly withstand the temptation of identifying the Amorite allies (Joshua x. 3) with the states which remained faithful to the Egyptian overlord.[20] States were bound together between themselves and singly with the Pharaoh by treaties, implying the taking of oaths and acceptance of responsibilities, such as we find described in Joshua ix.[21] The important position of Jerusalem in the letters is reflected in the dominant role played by the king of Jerusalem among the anti-Gibeonite allies, and the names of the respective kings are both formed with that of a deity worshipped in the pre-Israelite city.[22] We may cautiously suggest that these factors support a date for the events described in Joshua ix–x. 1–5 not too far removed from the Amarna period.

Before going on to discuss the contribution of Joshua ix to our knowledge of the early history of the Gibeonite cities we must take some time to examine the literary structure and composition of this chapter. That it has undergone successive editing is suggested at once by the description of the parties to the treaty: the 'leaders of the congregation' (*nᵉśî'ē hā'ēḏāh*) and the Israelites variously described as 'Israel' (verse 2), 'the men of Israel' (verses 6, 7), 'the sons of Israel' (verses 17, 18), 'the congregation' (*hā'ēḏāh*, verse 18) or simply 'the men' (verse 14) on the one hand; on the other, 'the inhabitants of Gibeon' (verse 3), 'the Hivites' (verse 7) and 'their elders' (verse 11). This would already lead us to suspect that the identity of the contracting party on the Israelite side was seen to be of importance throughout the editorial history of the chapter. Other examples of unevenness will be noted at once. The Gibeonites speak to Joshua and the men of Israel but only the latter answer (verses 6f.). Then Joshua asks the same question in different words (verse 8) and the Gibeonites respond with a set speech after which (*a*) *the men of Israel* partake of the stale bread, (*b*) *Joshua* makes peace with the Gibeonites and (*c*) *the leaders of the congregation* take the oath committing the Israelites to the treaty. Then in verse 22, just when the whole question seemed to have been settled, Joshua re-opens negotiations and from then on the leaders of the congregation are no longer mentioned.

The literary analysis of this chapter on the basis of Pentateuchal source-criticism has not resulted in any unanimity nor has it marshalled anything like the evidence required to make out a convincing case. In general, the continuation of J and E into the historical books has not proved its worth and is looked on with increasing and justified suspicion.[23] It is, however, clear that the narrative has undergone Deuteronomic editing.[24] The introduction (verses 1–2) is in line with Deuteronomic usage with respect to the division of the land (Deut. i.7) and the enumeration of indigenous populations (cf. Deut. xx.17, the same order). Rules for the conduct of the Holy War laid down in Deut. xx.10–18 provide the basic preamble for understanding the conduct of the Israelites faced with the Gibeonite petition for a treaty, especially with respect to distant cities (*ʿārîm rᵉḥōqôṯ*) which were to be spared but put to forced labour (*lāmas*). In Joshua ix.6 the Gibeonites claim to come from a distant land (*mēʾereṣ rᵉḥôqāh*) and they are put to forced labour, if of a special kind. Comparison with the fragmentary narrative contained in Judges ii.1–5 is instructive in this respect since it too has been edited by the Deuteronomists and deals with the baneful consequences of entering into alliance with the peoples of the land.[25]

In view of the fact that the Gibeonite treaty is concluded at the Benjaminite sanctuary of Gilgal (verse 6) the clear traces of a covenant-ceremony carried out at the same sanctuary which we find in Deut. xxvii are of particular interest.[26] As is generally recognized, this chapter contains a conflation of Shechemite and Gilgalite covenant tradition.[27] Joshua viii.30–5 clearly corresponds to the Shechemite tradition preserved in Deuteronomy and is followed immediately by the narrative of the treaty with the Gibeonites carried out at Gilgal. Since we can hardly suppose that the Gibeonite treaty is a literary fiction created by the Deuteronomists, this raises the question whether Gibeon in addition to Shechem may have contributed to the mainstream covenant tradition in the Old Testament.[28]

The Gibeonites are condemned to be 'hewers of wood and drawers of water' (verses 21, 23, 27), a class identified in Deut. xxix.10 with *gērîm* (*gērḵa 'ᵃšer bᵉqereḇ maḥᵃnēka*). The treaty narrative makes it clear that the Gibeonites are incorporated in the manner of *gērîm*. Joshua was obliged to rush to their assistance when they were attacked, but from 2 Sam. xxi.4 we gather that the Gibeonites were not able to apply the principle of blood feud.[29] Further indications of the Deuteronomist hand may be found in the reference to the Exodus (verses 9–10, 24) and campaigns east of the Jordan (verse 10; cf. Deut. ii.26ff.), the fourfold use of the adjective *bālāh* (verses 4–5; cf. Deut. viii.4 and xxix.4) and the final phrase 'in the place which he should choose' (verse 27; cf. Deut. xii.5, etc.).[30]

Many commentators have taken it for granted that this narrative, together with others in Joshua, has undergone Priestly redaction. This view is founded on the reference to the leaders of the congregation and their role in the negotiations as well as mention of 'the altar of Yahweh' (verse 27).[31] The association between the Gibeonites and the post-exilic *nethinim* is generally recalled at this point, and it may well be that post-exilic editors traced the origins of this group back to the treaty. We should, however, take note of the possibility that *'ēḏāh* may be a genuinely ancient term,[32] and the reference to the altar could be ascribed to the Deuteronomists.

As it stands, the narrative presents difficulties quite apart from the attempt to break it down into different sources. It seems hardly likely, for one thing, that the Israelites would allow themselves to be so easily fooled or would not have asked themselves why the Gibeonites, if they were emissaries from a far country, should have desired to enter into an alliance with them.[33] At one point the bread is presented simply to prove the length of their journey while a little later we find the Israelites partaking of it as part of the treaty-making. It is possible to detect, throughout the negotiations, a certain air of unreality and even detached humour especially with regard to the means chosen by the Gibeonites to authenticate their mission – as if anyone would believe that they could not have obtained fresh bread on the journey! Most commentators have noticed at least some of these oddities and inconsistencies in the story and have posited at least two narrative-strands. Möhlenbrink thinks of an earlier Gilgal version which made no mention of the fate of the Gibeonites and a later Shiloh narrative which described what happened to them.[34] Noth believes that one strand was aimed polemically against Benjamin because the tribe was guilty of illegitimate treaty-relationship with non-Israelite groups, and that the other was intended to explain the origins of a class of minor cultic personnel in the Jerusalem Temple.[35] For him the role of Joshua is secondary throughout, whereas Möhlenbrink does introduce him into his Shiloh strand. Hertzberg finds the basic narrative in verses 16–21*a*. To this narrative, which was favourable to the Gibeonites, there came to be added the story of the ruse featuring Joshua and reflecting anti-Benjaminite animus in Jerusalem at the time of Solomon.[36] Abel also finds two strands: one with Joshua and the men of Israel, the other of Priestly origin featuring the leaders of the congregation.[37] Others have applied different criteria or the same criteria with different results.[38]

It is not to our purpose to comment in detail on these different readings of the treaty narrative. For the moment it seems safe to assume that at least two factors have influenced the formation of the tradition behind this narrative: the need to justify Israelite tolerance of this ethnically alien group and/or to establish responsibility for making the treaty; the need to explain the origins of certain groups of minor cultic personnel operating in the Second (and possibly First) Temple.

To admit the existence of polemical overwriting and aetiological elements does not by any means imply doubt as to the essential historicity of the event described, namely, that a treaty was made between Israelites and Gibeonites. Confirmation is at hand since David's action during the famine (2 Sam. xxi. 1–14) is intelligible only on the supposition that his predecessor had violated such a treaty. Less certainly, we might also appeal to the assassination of Ishbaal son of Saul by men from a Gibeonite city (2 Sam. iv. 2ff.) since this action is best explained as vengeance for Saul's violation of the treaty.[39] Whether a further argument may be drawn from the results of the excavation at el-Jîb is doubtful and had better be left out of account.[40]

The description of how the treaty was made fits in closely with what we know of political treaties which have survived from the period in question. The term *kāraṯ berîṯ*, attested elsewhere in the north-west Semitic area, is used (verses 6, 7, 11, 15, 16), as is also the technical treaty-term *šālôm* (verse 15) implying at the least mutual non-aggression.[41] The Gibeonite emissaries refer to themselves as *ʿaḇāḏîm* of the Israelites (verse 8), thus clearly expressing their unequal status and further defining the kind of treaty they had in mind. Several protectorate treaties have survived from the Amarna period or close to it, and the same kind of treaty is presupposed by many of the Amarna letters themselves.[42] Other elements commonly found in this kind of treaty stand out clearly. The two parties share a meal (verse 14) and the elders swear an oath on behalf of the Israelites (verses 15, 18, 20; cf. 2 Sam. xxi. 2) – which no doubt explains why Yahweh himself came to the assistance of the threatened Gibeonites in the following battle.[43] The name of the tutelary deity on the Gibeonite side is, understandably enough, not given in the text.[44] The curses which were practically *de rigueur* in such treaties do not occur in Joshua ix but the famine which raged during the reign of David was interpreted as the result of a treaty-curse, parallel to what we find elsewhere.[45] The connection between Joshua ix and 2 Sam. xxi. 1–14 is further emphasized by the exposing of the corpses, in accord with the fate of treaty-violators elsewhere in the ancient Near East, and by the demand for retribution parallel with the retribution clause found in several Hittite treaties of that time.[46] We do not hear that the Gibeonite treaty was committed to writing but it is reasonable to suppose that it was; at all events, it was still in force and remembered at the time of David. Such a written copy may well have been deposited in the Gibeonite sanctuary (cf. Deut. xxxi. 25f.) at which, in all probability, David sought and received the oracle leading to the retribution visited on the descendants of Saul (2 Sam. xxi. 1).[47]

If we turn from Joshua ix to the narrative about the treaty between the sons of Jacob and the Shechemites in Gen. xxxiv we cannot help noting some interesting similarities. In both cases we have a situation of ethnic tension. The population around Shechem is described as Canaanite and Perizzite (Gen. xxxiv. 30) but a more precise indication is the reference to Hamor the Hivite who was prince of the land (verse 2).[48] The name Hamor itself may, as has often been pointed out, reflect a tradition of peaceful treaty relationship between groups settled in and around Shechem, and we have extra-biblical evidence of some degree of ethnic symbiosis in the city during the fourteenth century.[49] Though clearly in a position of superiority (verse 10), the Shechemites request a treaty of friendship with the sons of Jacob which would allow free inter-marriage between the two groups. This request is granted on condition of their accepting circumcision (verses 13ff.) but the treaty is violated by Simeon and Levi. Their attempt to exterminate the Shechemites was evidently not so successful as this account would give us to understand since, as a result at least in part of this action, the two tribes lost their predominance and had to move south.[50] In a similar manner Saul broke the treaty made earlier with the Gibeonites by attempting to exterminate them (or so the Gibeonites claimed, 2 Sam. xxi. 5), which violation contributed to his own downfall and that of his family.[51]

We may note, in addition, that although Hamor and Shechem negotiate the treaty it can be ratified only by 'the men of the city' (verse 20). These may well be the equivalent of the *ba'ᵃlê šᵉḵem* (Judges ix.2; cf. *ba'ᵃlê yᵉhûḏāh*, 2 Sam. vi.1) who accepted Abimelech as king and later rejected him. A similar collective action on the part of the men of Gibeon may be presumed since the term 'elders' (Joshua ix.11) is clearly influenced by Israelite usage and, as we have seen, no king is mentioned.

That the treaty between Shechem and the sons of Jacob is inserted into the history of the Patriarchs suggests that it took place at an early date, certainly previous to the main thrust of the settlement in the thirteenth century. Levi is here still a secular tribe and time has to be left for both of the tribes involved to retreat to the south and leave this part of the Central Highlands open to the penetration of the Joseph tribes.[52] In view of the rather impressive similarity between the events as described here and what we learn from some of the Amarna letters of the activity of '*apiru* in the Shechem region several scholars are prepared to read this chapter as a reflection of this activity.[53] Yet, as Harrelson points out, 'it would be rash to *identify* the sons of Hamor with Lab'ayu and his sons or Jacob and his family with the 'Apiru. The events are *comparable* but certainly not identical' (italics his).[54] But it would be reasonable to maintain that the incident is compatible with a date during or very close to the time of the Amarna letters, namely, the first half of the fourteenth century.

It was stated earlier in this chapter that, despite the close similarity between the Gibeonite–Israelite situation as set out in Joshua ix–x and the situation presupposed by the Amarna letters from Palestine, especially those from Jerusalem, we cannot easily date the treaty and coalition to that time. Abdi-ḫepa(t) is king of Jerusalem not Adonizedek (Joshua x.3); Zimredda rules in Lachish followed by Shipti-ba'alu and Iabni-ilu and there is no mention of a Japhia; Šuwardata is ruler of Hebron[55] not Hoham. We may add the Gezer dynasts Milki-ilu, Lapakhu and Ba'alu-shipti as opposed to Horam defeated by Joshua (x.33). The most probable hypothesis would be that the biblical events took place towards the end of or shortly after the Amarna period and not too long after the settlement of a Hivite group north-west of Jerusalem.

To accept this as a working hypothesis raises all sorts of questions for the date of the settlement of the tribes in Palestine, the originality of the role of Joshua and the connection between the account of the treaty and the events described as following upon it. Since the Gibeoniter cities were incorporated into Benjamin we would naturally be led to conclude that the treaty was made with Benjamin or with groups which later came to form the tribe of Benjamin. This, however, would not necessarily commit us to a date for the treaty in the thirteenth century since, admitting the evidence for widespread settlement in that century,[56] we must still allow for a much earlier date for the first penetration, of a more or less peaceful nature, of groups which the tradition has identified with the twelve-tribal structure.[57] As was argued a moment ago, this earlier date must be postulated for the events behind the tradition in Gen. xxxiv, and in view of the close association between Benjamin and the Joseph tribes a similar view is strongly suggested for the treaty with the Gibeonites in Joshua ix.[58] The role of the Ephraimite Joshua as war-leader seems so firmly established in the tradition that we can hardly avoid associating him with the decisive phase of the settlement in the thirteenth century and therefore detaching him from the account of the treaty and probably also from the campaign which is described in Joshua x.1–27.[59] The conquest of the south, the account of which follows on immediately (Joshua x.28–43), will in that case have been edited on to the narrative of the Battle of Gibeon and described as resulting from it.

A final difficulty in the treaty-narrative ought to be mentioned. In view of the earlier and more realistic account of the settlement contained in Judges i, where it is represented as a gradual and painful process, it must seem strange that Israel, *a fortiori* one tribe,[60] should succeed in imposing such a humiliating treaty on a 'great city' with a warlike reputation (Joshua x. 2). The difficulty is increased by the fact that in a protectorate or suzerainty treaty the oath was sworn by the inferior party whereas here it is the Israelites who swear (ix. 15).[61] Moreover, in the similar treaty made between the Shechemites and the sons of Jacob (Gen. xxxiv), the former request the treaty although they are clearly the stronger party and subsequently prove themselves to be so, as we may deduce from the disappearance of Simeon and Levi from that region. We need hardly insist that the account of the Conquest in Joshua i–xii is written from the later standpoint of the twelve-tribal league and redacted *ad maiorem gloriam Israel*, as a comparison with Judges i will at once reveal. We must therefore reckon with the strong possibility that this is one case, not the only one, of groups later to form part of Israel which established initially peaceful relationships with much stronger and better established political entities in the early stages of penetration into Palestine.

## CHAPTER IV

# THE BATTLE OF GIBEON AND ITS SEQUEL

In the biblical text the battle is described as the immediate outcome of the concerted attack on Gibeon by the Amorite allies and this attack as directly occasioned by the treaty. Before enquiring whether this represents the actual course of events we need to take a closer look at the literary composition and history of Joshua x as a whole.

The narrative begins by speaking of the reaction provoked among neighbouring city-states by the Israelite–Gibeonite treaty. Adonizedek king of Jerusalem placed himself at the head of a coalition of five Amorite cities which proceeded to launch an attack on Gibeon (verses 1–5). In response to the Gibeonites' urgent plea for assistance Joshua marched from Gilgal and inflicted a crushing defeat on the allies (verses 6–15). The fate of the five kings is then described in detail (verses 16–27) and this is followed by a summary account of the Israelite conquest, under Joshua's leadership, of 'the hill country, the Negeb, the lowlands and the slopes', that is, of the whole of the South (verses 28–43).

The analysis of Joshua x on the basis of Pentateuchal source-criticism is, on the whole, no more convincing than in the previous chapter.[1] In both cases we must begin with what positive structural and stylistic elements can be discerned. The chapter falls naturally into three parts: the coalition and campaign, the fate of the five kings, the summary of Joshua's campaigns in the south. Whether this division corresponds to three originally distinct sources can be determined, if at all, only after a closer look at the composition of each part. Among recent scholars G. E. Wright appears to be the only one to defend the unity of the chapter.[2] Almost all concede that the aetiological narrative about the fate of the five kings has had a separate existence. Since, however, this in no way contributes to our knowledge of the history of Gibeon we may leave it aside.[3]

As is clear from verses 1–2, the first section is closely related to the account of the treaty. This at once raises an important issue for the assessment of the whole chapter as historical source-material, for if the coalition is understood to follow immediately after the treaty it becomes so much more difficult to dissociate the battle from the preceding events. In view of the fact that the treaty is independently attested by the narrative in 2 Sam. xxi. 1–14 we can hardly follow Gressmann and Sellin in supposing that the treaty is an unhistorical prelude to the military action described in the following chapter.[4] In view of the present understanding of the literary history of Joshua as a whole it would seem more logical to suspect that the campaign has been antedated to the earliest days of the settlement of Benjamin – especially if the analogy with Gen. xxxiv, discussed in the preceding chapter, is accepted.[5]

Of great importance in this discussion is the role attributed to Joshua in both the treaty and the subsequent events. In the preceding chapter serious difficulties were raised against the historicity of Joshua's role in the treaty negotiations. Equally serious reasons exist for scepticism concerning the part allotted to him in the campaign and battle which follow: the great theological importance which he has in the Deuteronomist scheme of history,[6] the pervasive presence of Holy War 'ideology' in this chapter (to be discussed shortly), the improbable return to the camp at Gilgal in verse 15,[7] the absence of any reference to him in the quotation from the Book of Yashar.[8] As against this view, Alt argued that the battle near Gibeon is an Ephraimite *Heldensage* in which the role of Joshua the *Held* from Ephraim is not expendable.[9] The decisive location was Beth-horon in Ephraim (Joshua xviii. 13 places it on the Benjaminite boundary) and the mention of Gibeon in the prose narrative is part of the editorial work involved in linking this chapter with the preceding. What really happened was an encounter between Israelites and Canaanites with Joshua at the head of the Joseph tribes or perhaps of Ephraim alone. A serious objection to this view is that the verse fragment (verses 12*b*–13*a*) mentions Gibeon and Aijalon but not Beth-horon and verse 10 states clearly that the *makkāh gᵉḏôlāh* took place at Gibeon. Beth-horon lies on the only available access- and escape-route between the Central Highlands and the Coastal Plain and features in several other military episodes referred to in both the Old Testament and the Amarna letters.[10] Its place in the present narrative obviously derives from the importance of the pursuit in the context of the Holy War, an aspect of the problem which Alt appears to have overlooked. Hence the fact that Beth-horon is in Ephraim hardly provides an adequate basis for this interpretation of the episode. Moreover, even if Joshua is thought of as an Ephraimite *charismatischer Führer*, it does not thereby follow that his activities were limited to his own tribe.

A further problem which confronts us at once is that of relating this narrative to the early traditions found in Judges i. At first sight, Judges i.4ff. looks like a Judahite version of Joshua x.1ff. The sphere of operations is identical in both cases (cf. Joshua ix.1; x.40 with Judges i.9) and three of the cities which are taken and destroyed by Joshua in Joshua x are captured by Judahites in Judges i.[11] Despite the variant reading of LXX$^{BA}$ in Joshua x.1 we are justified in reading 'Adonizedek' both here and in Judges i.5ff. Both are described as king of Jerusalem and no satisfactory explanation for the form 'Adonibezek' is known.[12]

The glaring discrepancies between the two accounts are clearly the outcome of polemical re-editing of old tradition respectively by a Benjaminite (or Ephraimite) and Judahite hand. To what extent both were prepared to go can be seen in the claim advanced by both to have captured Jerusalem. This addiction to polemical re-editing must be held responsible for much of the obscurity surrounding Gibeon at the time of the Israelite settlement and the period which followed it. It also makes a comparative study of the two texts extremely difficult. Not only are there inconsistencies within each (e.g. concerning Makkedah in Joshua x and Jerusalem in Judges i) but also fairly obvious contradictions between the two (e.g. Gezer is taken by Joshua in Joshua x.33; the Ephraimites attempt unsuccessfully to take it in Judges i.29). Hence we need to be acutely aware of the polemical slant before attempting to use these narratives as source-material.[13]

For the purposes of this study it will not be necessary to discuss whether originally only one king rather than the five named participated in the campaign.[14] We saw earlier that the names, which sound perfectly genuine, coincide in no case with names of Canaanite rulers known from the Amarna correspondence.

Several difficulties have been advanced against both the unity and historical credibility of the campaign narrative as a whole. Some see it as resulting from the conflation of two sources since there appear to be two different indications of the route taken by the fleeing confederates and two distinct causes for their defeat.[15] In verse 10*b* the Amorites flee 'as far as Azekah and Makkedah' and in verse 11*a* 'from the Ascent of Beth-horon'. In view of the location of Azekah and Makkedah, well south of the well-trodden 'way of Beth-horon', it is not impossible that this indication comes from the editor who inserted the Makkedah tradition (verses 16–28).[16] As for the means by which the victory was accomplished, there need be no incompatibility between the preternaturally large and destructive hailstones and the solar phenomenon. The former has to do with the battle itself, the latter with the pursuit and complete destruction of the enemy. Read within the context of the Holy War, these are distinct phases which must not be confused.

The actual battle is described in terms familiar from other Holy War episodes, raising an important issue which we shall discuss later in this chapter. The quotation from the Book of Yashar (verses 12*b*–13*a*), which is surely of genuine antiquity,[17] is followed by what appears to be a prose paraphrase (verse 13*b*) though here too there is a strong rhythmic element:

*ya'ᵃmōḏ haššemeš baḥᵃṣî haššāmayim*
*wᵉlō'-'āṣ lāḇô' kᵉyôm tāmîm.*[18]

The juxtaposition of prose- and verse-narrative of the same event is found elsewhere in the Old Testament; in particular, the Song at the Papyrus Sea (Exod. xv. 1–18) together with the preceding prose-narrative (xiv. 15–31) and the Song of Deborah (Judges v; cf. iv). The former is also introduced by the 'heroic adverb' *'āz* (cf. Joshua x. 12) which occurs often[19] in Judges v and introduces other poetic fragments in Num. xxi. 17 and 1 Kings viii. 12, the latter also from the Book of Yashar according to LXX.[20] The fact that verses 12*b*–13*a* (if not also 13*b*) come from a collection represented elsewhere in the Old Testament makes it necessary to consider the quotation and the context in which it is placed separately.

In the first place, the interpretation of the quotation, as given in verses 12*a* and 13*b*–14, is clear. Joshua asks Yahweh in the presence of the Israelite army for time to complete the pursuit and annihilation of the enemy, and this is granted when the sun remains high in the sky for a whole day (or, the remainder of the day). This is how the incident has generally been understood in Jewish tradition (e.g. Ecclus. xlvi. 4–6) and in the Christian churches. And even if it is assumed that verses 12–14 were originally independent of the present narrative or belong elsewhere,[21] reference is certainly made to an action in or near Gibeon.

The quotation itself is limited to verses 12*b*–13*a*, though in view of the difficult and prosodically irregular *'ad̲ yiqqōm gôy 'ōyᵉb̲āw*[22] verse 13*a* has sometimes been read as an addition in verse explanatory of verse 12*b*, especially in view of the similar *wᵉniqqamtî mē'ōyᵉb̲āy* in 1 Sam. xiv. 24.[23] The fragment itself remains difficult of interpretation not only because we know nothing about the Book of Yashar apart from the two, possibly three, quotations from it in the Old Testament, but also because we do not know whether this particular fragment was part of a longer composition or was originally situated in a different context. We must at least take note of some apparent discrepancies between the quotation considered in itself and the context in which it is situated.

(i) Whereas in the latter Joshua addresses Yahweh, the quotation contains an invocation addressed by an unnamed speaker directly to the sun and moon.[24]

(ii) The verb *'āmaḏ* is used of the sun in the quotation, *dāṃaṃ* in the commentary (verse 13*b*).

(iii) The moon is not referred to in the prose setting though such a reference might have been expected from its occurrence in the quotation. This, however, would not necessarily lead to the conclusion that *yārēaḥ* is simply a ballast word due to synonymous parallelism.[25]

(iv) In the quotation the sun is *b^e gibʿôn* not, as we would have expected, *'al gibʿôn*, and the moon *b^e ʿēmeq 'ayyālôn*. The presumption is that they are both simultaneously visible. In the prose setting the sun is *baḥ^a ṣî haššāmayim*, that is, at its zenith, when presumably the moon would be invisible.

These considerations suggest that we take account of the possibility that the quotation is not native to this context.

Numerous hypotheses have been advanced over the years in explanation of verses 12*b*–13*a* which, for the purposes of this study, it will not be necessary to evaluate singly and in detail.[26] The literary form of the couplet (verse 12*b*), which is apostrophe or address, suggests a prayer or, more likely, an incantation or spell the interpretation of which depends on the meaning of the imperative *dôm* (cf. *yaʿ^a mōḏ*, verse 13*b*). The connotation 'to be dark', 'not to shine', has often been suggested; but against this is the fact that there is no evidence for this meaning either in the Old Testament or the Ugaritic texts.[27] More commonly the sense 'to stand still', 'to be silent' is suggested. Of the thirty occurrences of *dāmam* in the Old Testament thirteen refer to the latter and six to the former, with the remainder uncertain.[28] We should add that in several of these examples both connotations, which are in any case closely allied, may be present. According to Driver, *dm* (*dmy*) occurs four times in the Ugaritic texts with the meaning 'be quiet, still, silent'.[29] Where the emphasis is placed will evidently depend in good part on the interpretation of the passage as a whole.[30]

Widely overlooked in the long discussion on the meaning

of the verbs used is the occurrence of both (*dāmam* and ‘*āmad*) together in 1 Sam. xiv. 9, also in a Holy War context. Jonathan is preparing for his attack on the Philistines and instructs his armour-bearer on how to proceed in the imminent action:

> If they say to us, ‘wait (*dōmmû*) until we come to you’ then we will stand still (‘*āmadnû*) in our place and we will not go up to them (*na*‘*ᵃleh*).

From this we may infer that *dāmam* can have the meaning of non-participation in battle, the opposite of ‘*ālāh*, attack. This is clearly the closest parallel in the Old Testament the relevance of which should be considered before turning to more distant analogies.[31] The inference would be that the two verbs are parallel in meaning and that verse 12*b* may be an abjuration addressed to sun and moon not to take part in the military action resulting in the destruction of Yahweh's enemies.

Can this meaning be further defined and defended in the context of the quotation itself? Recently Heller and Dus have suggested that the ŠMŠ addressed is a solar deity worshipped at Gibeon.[32] According to both authors, the couplet had no original reference to Joshua's campaign but was an incantation recited in the Israelite sanctuary of Gibeon after the tutelary deity of the city had been made subject to Yahweh. Dus believes he can find confirmation of ŠMŠ-worship by the Gibeonites in certain place-names formed with -ŠMŠ in the immediate locality, the conspicuous place given to solar worship in the Jerusalem cult (especially 1 Kings viii. 12) and a comparison between the ritual execution of the Saulites at Gibeon (2 Sam. xxi. 1–14) and that of the apostate Israelites at Baal-peor (Num. xxv. 1–5). Before appraising the positive and constructive elements of this hypothesis it must, however, be noted that it is vitiated by the failure to take seriously the tradition about a treaty of friendship between Gibeonites and some groups which were later to form part of Israel. If these authors are correct in supposing that the apostrophe is addressed to a deity,[33] as seems form-critically and historically quite feasible, this must be in the sense that only Yahweh is to intervene in the military action though both he and the Gibeonite deity (deities?) had been invoked in the treaty.[34]

Caution is in order with respect to the essential element in this hypothesis, the existence of ŠMŠ-worship among the Gibeonites. Archaeological evidence is slight and of doubtful interpretation. A royal seal with the winged sun-disc and what may be a representation of the solar charioteer was discovered during the excavation of el-Jîb.[35] An inscribed seal found in the valley of Aijalon has been interpreted as representing the adoration of the sun-child Horus and with this a scarab inscribed *ḥr thnw*, found at el-Jîb, may be compared.[36] These would most naturally suggest Egyptian influence. The place-names adduced by Dus occur in the territory of Dan not Benjamin though none is far distant from el-Jîb.[37] Significantly, Samson (*šimšôn*) is also a Danite. Close associations between Gibeonites and Beth-shemeshites may perhaps be deduced from 1 Sam. vi. 19ff. and find some confirmation in the excavations.[38] Beth-horon, where the final annihilation took place, can hardly be dissociated from the Egypto-Canaanite solar deity Horon (Ḥaurôn).[39]

The evidence for solar worship in Jerusalem during the time of the monarchy is real enough but ought not to be exaggerated; and in any case it is not so easy to say what influence was predominant in producing it.[40] If it may be traced back to the pre-Israelite period the association between Gibeon and Jerusalem, especially with regard to the cultic tradition, would certainly increase the probability of solar worship among the Gibeonites, though any conclusions drawn on this basis will clearly be hypothetical. As for Dus's comparison between 2 Sam. xxi. 1–14 and Num. xxv. 1–5, we may at least admit that there are some striking points of resemblance between the two narratives. In both cases the execution is a ritual act performed 'before Yahweh' (Num. xxv. 4; 2 Sam. xxi. 6). The manner of the killing is expressed in the obscure verb *hôqîaʿ* which is found only in these two texts.[41] At Peor the action has to be performed *neged haššemeš* (verse 4), and in 2 Sam. xxi. 6 LXX translates the obscure Hebrew verb with ἐξηλιάσωμεν which Liddell and Scott take to mean 'to set in the sun; to crucify or hang in the open air' but to which Heller gives the further meaning of a rite in honour of the sun god.[42] With respect to this last point, we can only remark on the oddity of Moses executing the apostate Israelites in honour of the sun god on account of their turning to the Baal of Peor. The comparison may still be relevant, as we shall shortly see, but for a rather different reason.

Presuming a Hurrian or Hurrian-related presence at Gibeon and its cities it would be logical and only fair to this hypothesis to enquire what place solar worship had among the Hurrians of the cuneiform inscriptions. By the last days of the Hittite Empire the great sun-goddess Arinna had been fully identified with Ḫepat. She was the supreme patroness of the empire and her assistance in battle was looked for as a matter of course.[43] She is also found in association with the Hurrian *Gewittergott* one of whose functions was to protect the king during battle and in general further his cause.[44] A male solar deity Shimike also occurs in some texts, and he may be the solar deity invoked by king Muwatallis. The relationship between the male and female solar deities is not clear.[45] The letter of Tushratta, a primary source for our knowledge of the Hurrians, contains the prayer that Amenophis III be protected by ŠMŠ and Ishtar, and personal names from Alalakh show that ŠMŠ (*Šapš*) and the Hurrian moon-god *Kušaḫ* were venerated there.[46] Since in addition the solar deity is almost always invoked in the treaties known to us, and in a prominent manner in those involving Hittites and Hurrians,[47] there would be nothing strange in the Gibeonites *qua* Hivites appealing to him both in the treaty and the military impasse in which they found themselves as a result of it.

The execution of the apostates 'in the sun before Yahweh' at Peor (or Beth-peor, Deut. iii. 29) raises an interesting problem with regard to our theme which cannot be solved in the present state of our knowledge but is worthy of mention nonetheless. This Moabite place-name has no known Semitic derivation but is essentially identical with the place-name *p*ʿ*r* occurring in the bilingual inscription from Karatepe to be identified with the residence of Urikki king of Que (Kizzuwatna).[48] According to Num. xxii.4–5 Balak ben-Zippor king of Moab sent for Balaam ben-Beor at Pethor, which can hardly be other than the Pitru known from Assyrian records and located in the extreme north of Syria. The fact that *ṣprm* occurs in the Karatepe inscription as an element in the name of a deity increases the probability of association between these traditions and the region of Kizzuwatna in which the majority of the population was of Hittite–Luvian and Hurrian stock.[49] Moreover, the same place-name φαγωρ < *p‘r*) occurs in the amplified LXX version of the Judahite city-list (Joshua xv.59) between Ephrath and Kiriath-jearim, both of which were originally in Benjamin as we have seen. These data, of uncertain interpretation as they are, may well indicate some connection in the history of the tradition between Num. xxv.1–5 and 2 Sam. xxi.1–14 and provide a further clue to the origins and ethnic composition of the Gibeonite enclave.[50]

The view that 2 Sam. xxi.1–14 reflects the Canaanite fertility myth in which ŠMŠ plays a distinctive role will be considered in a later chapter. We take the view that the ŠMŠ addressed was a solar deity venerated at Gibeon and invoked by them in the treaty and that the apostrophe is an enjoinder to remain inactive leaving the issue in the hands of Yahweh. Rather than regard *yārēaḥ* as merely a parallelism-word we would prefer to think of it as a lunar deity, perhaps the preferential cult of the city of Aijalon.[51]

We now return to the campaign narrative as a whole. There can be little doubt, in the first place, that the episode is narrated in terms of the Holy War: the injunction not to fear, the fear and panic of the enemy, the miraculous intervention of Yahweh suggest this quite clearly.[52] Other Holy War episodes which are recorded as taking place in the same region might be mentioned here. The account (1 Sam. xiv) of Jonathan's surprise attack on the Philistines, which we have seen to contain the two controversial verbs *dāmam* and *‘āmaḏ* in the same context as in Joshua x.13, has the same general character.

There is the request for an oracle (verses 18, 41), the ascription of the victory to Yahweh (verse 23), and the phrase *bayyôm hahû'* occurs four times.[53] The main emphasis is not on the battle so much as on the pursuit, obviously because of the theological importance of the *ḥērem*, and the cause of the enemy's undoing is a divinely inspired panic accompanied by miraculous phenomena (verses 15, 20). The action takes place near Michmash and Geba, that is, about five miles from Gibeon.[54] The retreat is down the valley of Aijalon (verse 13) which must have taken the Philistines past Gibeon – especially if we read Beth-horon for Beth-aven in verse 23.[55]

The second of the two victories of David over the Philistines (2 Sam. v. 17–25) is also described as taking place near Gibeon on the basis of the original reading *miggib̲'ôn* in verse 25. Here too there is the request for an oracle (verse 23) and the victory is accomplished by Yahweh marching to the assistance of his army through the tree-tops.[56] Similarly in 1 Sam. vii. 7–12 the victory of Samuel is brought about by the divinely inspired panic (verse 10) accompanied by thunder (the voice of Yahweh).[57] Here too we find the 'heroic' *bayyôm hahû'* (verse 10) and the mandatory annihilation of the enemy. The retreat passes through Beth-car (verse 11), a place-name otherwise unknown. Many commentators have accepted Klostermann's emendation to Beth-horon,[58] especially since once again the most natural retreat-route would have been down the valley of Aijalon. If, as suggested in an earlier chapter, we identify the Mizpah of this narrative with el-Jîb, the locality is identical with that in Joshua x. 1–14. We may finally, with some hesitation, include for consideration the account of Benjamin's defeat by the tribal levy in Judges xx. 14–48. Here, as in 1 Sam. xiv, a sacred fast is ordained before the battle (verses 20, 26), there is an oath (xxi. 1), consulting for an oracle (xx. 18, 23, 27) and the building of an altar afterwards (xxi. 4). The victory is ascribed to Yahweh though nothing is said of a miraculous intervention. The completion of the *ḥērem* is clearly of importance (xx. 32ff.) and *bayyôm hahû'* occurs several times (xx. 15, 21, 35, 46). Emending *gib̲'āṯāh* to *gib̲'ônāh* in xx.31 would also place the episode in the same locality as Joshua x.1–14.[59]

Implicitly in Num. x.35f. and explicitly in several episodes in Joshua and 1–2 Sam. the ark is associated with the Holy War.[60] In 1 Sam. iv.4f. the arrival of the ark on the battlefield is followed by the shaking of the earth and in v.9, 11 the divinely inspired panic is attributed explicitly to it. In 1 Sam. iv.5 and in the theologically highly coloured account of the capture of Jericho (Joshua vi.10, 16, 20) the *t^erû'āh* or acclamation is linked with the presence of the ark. Though historically reliable evidence for the taking of the ark into battle is available only from the time of the Philistine war (1 Sam. iv.3ff. and 2 Sam. xi.11), Num. x.35ff. would lead us to suppose that this was an older practice. With respect to the Holy War episodes discussed above, the only explicit reference to the ark is in Judges xx.27. By general consent this belongs to the latest strand of the narrative yet confirms the theological or ideological association between Holy War and ark. In 1 Sam. vii.7–12 the engagement with the Philistines at Mizpah follows immediately upon the installation of the ark at Kiriath-jearim and it is implied that the source of the miraculous phenomena is the divine presence in the sanctuary.[61] Hence it would not be unreasonable to conclude, despite the uncertainty which shrouds the early history of the ark, that this kind of terminology found in the passages discussed above owes something to the tradition concerning the ark's sojourn among the Gibeonites.

CHAPTER V

# THE GIBEONITE CITIES DURING THE PERIOD OF THE JUDGES AND THE REIGN OF SAUL

After the narrative of the treaty and its immediate outcome (Joshua ix–x; xi. 19) we find no further mention of any of the Gibeonite cities until we come to the account of the transference of the ark from Beth-shemesh to Kiriath-jearim (1 Sam. vi. 21 – vii. 2).[1] After the account of the meeting at the pool of Gibeon (2 Sam. ii. 12ff.) and the assassination of Ishbaal by two Beerothites (2 Sam. iv. 2ff.) there occurs no further mention until the last stage of the ark's progress (2 Sam. vi. 1ff.) preceded by the defeat of the Philistines 'from Gibeon (LXX and Chron.) to Gezer' (v. 25). We may presume that the execution of the descendants of Saul at Gibeon (2 Sam. xxi. 1–14) took place during the early years of David's reign. Consequently, all that the tradition tells us for the period in question is that the ark was left in a Gibeonite city for a period of 'some twenty years' (1 Sam. vii. 2).

During this same period we hear of the ark at Bethel (Judges xx. 27) and at Shiloh (1 Sam. iii. 3; iv. 4) whence it was taken into battle and lost to the Philistines. After 1 Sam. vii. 2, however, there is no further reference to it until the account of its transference to Jerusalem in 2 Sam. vi. 2ff.[2] This covers the period from shortly after the fall of Shiloh to the early years of David's reign, a period which must certainly have been longer than the 'twenty years' of 1 Sam. vii. 2. As is generally recognized, 1 Sam. vii. 2–17 is a late composition and generally untrustworthy as a historical source for the period.[3] It manifests clear signs of Deuteronomic editing, and twenty years or a multiple of twenty occurs frequently in historical narratives which bear the Deuteronomist stamp (e.g. Judges xv. 20; xvi. 31). The period must include the phase of Philistine domination down to the beginning of Saul's reign, all the reign of the latter and the early part of David's reign down to the transference of the ark. This last cannot be determined with certainty since, *inter alia*, we do not know whether the seven and a half years of David's reign at Hebron (2 Sam. v.5) overlapped with Saul's reign.

The imponderable element is, of course, the length of Saul's reign. 1 Sam. xiii.1 (M.T.) is corrupt and grammatically unfeasible as it stands.[4] Some Greek minuscules have 'thirty years' and a later Jewish tradition speaks of a reign of forty years.[5] A careful study of the traditions about Saul suggests a period considerably in excess of two years. His manifold military activities, his proceedings against non-Israelite groups such as the Gibeonites, David's stay of one year and four months with the Philistines (1 Sam. xxvii.2) the ages attributed to his children,[6] his own psychological and religious evolution (however subjective a reconstruction of it may be) – these all suggest a considerably longer period. His association with groups outside Palestine, the names attributed to his family and descendants and the connection made by the Chronicler between his family and the Gibeonites (all of which will be discussed later in this chapter) suggest that, at the outset, Saul may have been no more Israelite than some of the other 'judges'.[7] At any rate, Saul did become an ardent Yahwist at least as early as the initial defeat of the Philistines (1 Sam. xiv). His zeal for Yahweh, referred to in 2 Sam. xxi.2, is evidenced by his waiting seven days for the tardy Samuel (1 Sam. xiii.8ff.), his insistence on the death of his son for breaking a religious taboo (xiv.37ff.) and the expulsion of the mediums and wizards (xxviii.9). It may have been this same zeal, allied with obvious political considerations, which led him to take action against the Gibeonites. It seems that a considerable period of time must be allowed for to explain the religious and psychological nadir which he reached towards the end of his life (see especially 1 Sam. xxviii.6ff.); and we might note in this connection that while his first son, Jonathan, bears a good Yahwist name, later sons have names formed with Baal.[8]

In the light of these considerations it would be reasonable to suggest that the text of 1 Sam. xiii. 1 has been altered, and it may be further suggested that this alteration was the result of a polemical attitude towards him evidenced fairly clearly elsewhere. The same factor may well be responsible for the two years also allotted to Ishbaal in 2 Sam. ii. 10. For Saul a reign of nine, twelve or twenty years has been suggested.[9] If we must assign a date in the middle of the eleventh century for the destruction of Shiloh,[10] and if David's reign dates from ca. 1000 B.C., we have a period of at least half a century for the sojourn of the ark in a Gibeonite city.[11]

That the Old Testament historical tradition is silent on the ark during this period may not at first sight seem to call for an explanation. Maier takes the view that it was not considered of great importance at this time and was simply neglected,[12] a view which is substantially in accord with the Chronicler (1 Chron. xiii. 3). Those who suppose that it ceased to be thought of as the central cult-object of the tribal federation do not adduce any evidence from the tradition in support of their contention, nor do they explain why David should have attached such importance to bringing it into his new religious cult-centre.[13] In his *The History of Israel*, Noth simply states that the Philistines took it as a pledge of their control over the tribes who thereafter took no more notice of it.[14] Similarly Bright states, without further comment, that it lay neglected for a generation or more at Kiriath-jearim, though he clearly sees its transference to Jerusalem as of vital importance.[15]

The problem of the silence about the ark at this time stands out in sharper profile if we note its occurrence in 1–2 Sam. in a purely statistical way. In 1 Sam. i–iii, the Shiloh narrative, it is mentioned only once, in a subordinate clause (iii. 3). The following narrative (iv. 1*b* – vii. 1), which is a more or less continuous composition, differs from i–iii very noticeably in style, and in general seems to be a later composition.[16] The centre of interest is here very definitely the ark which is mentioned thirty-five times under five different designations.[17] After the reference to the ark in the Mizpah narrative (vii. 2) there is complete silence until the history of its vicissitudes is resumed in 2 Sam. vi.1–19 where it occurs fourteen times, equally divided between *’$^{a}$rôn YHWH* and *’$^{a}$rôn ’$^{e}$lōhîm*. During the intervening period there is no reference to it at all despite the fact that it would almost certainly have been accessible to the followers of Saul after the victory recorded in 1 Sam. xiv.[18] We would therefore agree with those commentators who have seen a problem worthy of further investigation here,[19] and would suggest that this investigation must also take account of the absence, *for the same period*, of any reference in the tradition to Gibeon and its cities. Let us recall, once again, the political and cultic importance of Gibeon, attested for the period from the Settlement of the tribes to the time of Solomon (Joshua x.2; 1 Kings iii.4) and reflected in the work of the Chronicler and rabbinical tradition. To this we may add its obvious strategic significance during the Philistine war which was going on intermittently during the reign of Saul. Saul attacked one, and possibly several, of the Gibeonite cities (2 Sam. xxi.1ff.; iv.3), on account no doubt of the fact that this enclave cut his kingdom in half – quite apart from the possibility of collusion between Gibeonites and Philistines.[20] If the association between the ark and the kingship of Yahweh is not just the theologoumenon of a later age,[21] it would be difficult to suppose that Saul simply neglected it. David clearly did not.

One factor which is immediately relevant to our discussion is the polemical attitude discernible in the editing of many of these historical narratives. Thus, Judges xvii–xxi appears to have been edited by a pro-monarchist and Judahite writer, to judge by the recurrent comment, ‘in those days there was no king in Israel’ (xvii.6; xviii.1; xix.1; xxi.25). Judah is divinely appointed to lead the tribal levy against Benjamin (xx.18) and the possibility must be entertained that the narrative has been redacted to reflect an event or events during the reign of Saul – with clearly unfavourable implications.[22] In view of the fact that the Gibeonite cities are located in Benjamin, the anti-Benjaminite animus apparent in xix–xx is particularly significant.[23] We recall that much of the opposition to David came from Benjaminites (e.g. 2 Sam. vi.20ff.; xvi.5ff.; xx.1ff.) and that David himself progressively eliminated the descendants of the Benjaminite Saul (2 Sam. iii.22; iv.1ff.; xxi.1ff.; xvi.1ff.). All this is narrated with a strong emphasis on David's innocence and non-complicity designed, not altogether successfully, to dispel suspicion.

The disputed situation of Rachel's tomb provides indirect evidence of the same attitude. The earliest references place it in Benjamin (1 Sam. x.2; cf. Jer. xxxi.15) but the Yahwist narrator places it in Bethlehem (Gen. xxxv.19; xlviii.7) within the borders of Judah.[24] Other examples of the transference of traditions to Judah and, in particular, to Jerusalem, may be suggested if not proved. By the time of the Chronicler, for example, *hmryh* of Gen. xxii.2 has been identified with the site of the Solomonic temple (2 Chron. iii.1).[25] It is quite clear, at any rate, that despite David's appeasement of the Gibeonites the 'great high place' of Gibeon would not be allowed for long to challenge the new cult-centre in Jerusalem. This political exigency has surely influenced the form in which the traditions concerning the pre-monarchical period have been mediated to us. It may also help to explain the silence concerning both Gibeon and the ark for the period referred to and the textual confusion in many of the references to *gib̲ʿôn*, *gib̲ʿāh*, *haggib̲ʿāh*, etc.

Some of these polemical lines would, in all probability, have been further strengthened by the Deuteronomists. As the most prestigious high place of the early monarchical period Gibeon would hardly have escaped, so that even in the generally favourable notice on Solomon a note of disapproval can be heard for his visit to this sanctuary.[26] That alliances with the autochthonous populations are to be avoided is, moreover, a cardinal point of Deuteronomic law and a basic criterion of moral evaluation in the Deuteronomist history (e.g. Deut. vii.2; Judges ii.2). As has been seen, this has influenced the account of the treaty-making in Joshua ix and would reflect unfavourably on the tribe of Benjamin. In their attitude to the monarchy the Deuteronomists rarely go beyond cautious approval and are often condemnatory. Following on Hosea in particular, the aberration of Israel is traced back to the establishment of monarchy which would obviously reflect unfavourably on Saul and explain the presentation of Samuel as a paradigm of prophetic opposition to the monarchy.[27] We may note, further, that in all probability the account of the ritual execution of the descendants of Saul (2 Sam. xxi.1–14) did not form part of the Deuteronomist historical corpus but was brought into the narrative-complex at a later stage and out of chronological order.[28] It is therefore not altogether surprising that there is no reference to Saul in M.T. outside the historical narratives in 1–2 Sam. and 1 Chron. with the exception of one or two psalm-titles and the place-name Gibeah of Saul in Isa. x.29.

The almost complete absence of any direct information on the Gibeonites and their cities for this period and the polemical editing of the traditions which have survived make it urgent to ask whether anything may be concluded indirectly from this tradition or from any other sources. We may begin with Saul's attempt to eliminate this non-Israelite enclave, attested clearly in 2 Sam. xxi.1–2, 5. We have already seen that his action involved the inhabitants not just of Gibeon but of Beeroth as well, and probably of all the Gibeonite region.[29] At this point, however, we come up against a problem which so far has received insufficient attention. Indications within the biblical tradition which, though indirect, cannot easily be set aside, suggest a close association between Saul's family and Gibeon. According to 1 Sam. ix.1 Saul was the son of a fifth-generation Benjaminite. We would have expected to find here some reference to his place of origin, which is given in the case of much less prominent figures, but there is none. We will find him later established at Gibeah which appears to have been his capital for part of the reign,[30] but this says nothing about his place of origin. A surer indication is the family burial-site and this was 'in the land of Benjamin, in Zela' where the tomb of Kish his father was located (2 Sam. xxi.13f.). Zela is probably to be identified with the city of the same name in the

Benjaminite city-list (Joshua xviii.28) situated at Khirbet Ṣalah less than a mile from Nebi Samwil;[31] and this location would agree very well with the Chronicler's Saulite genealogy which is within that of the Gibeonites (1 Chron. viii.29–40). If the place-name *giḇʿaṯ hāʾᵉlōhîm* (1 Sam. x.5, 10; cf. xiii.3), where a Philistine garrison was located, may be identified with Gibeon (and we have seen this to be possible), the case would be strengthened even further. Saul was certainly well known there (see 1 Sam. x.11) and it was there that his uncle lived.[32]

Though many conclusions will doubtless be hypothetical, a brief survey of personal names in Saul's family may well prove instructive. Scattered throughout 1–2 Sam. we find some twenty-eight names of Saulites, there are twenty-four in the Chronicler's genealogy (1 Chron. viii.33–40 with some alternative forms in ix.39–44) and 1 Chron. xii.1–7 lists twenty-three of the 'brethren of Saul' who, however, may not be blood-relations. As with the Gibeonite names in 1 Chron. discussed earlier we may suppose, in the absence of proof to the contrary, that these names are for the most part genuine and not invented by the post-exilic author. Bearing in mind the uncertainties attending this kind of study, we may at least put forward some tentative conclusions.

It may, in the first place, be significant that six Saulite names, including that of Saul himself, occur among the Edomite names in Gen. xxxvi;[33] this especially in view of the interesting coincidence between Gibeonite and Edomite names referred to earlier.[34] The gentilic formed from Saul also occurs in the Negeb belonging to a group which contained a Canaanite (i.e. non-Israelite) admixture (Gen. xlvi.10); one of several cases of coincidence between personal and place names from the regions east of the Jordan, the Gibeonite region and the Negeb.[35] The name lacks a known theophoric element and no satisfactory Israelite derivation has been suggested.[36] In an earlier chapter we expressed reserve concerning the Arabic derivation of the name in Gen. xxxvi.37f.[37] The name of Saul's father Kish is likewise a matter of conjecture. Nöldeke compared it with *qyšʾ* of the Hiğr inscription and even suggested that this person may have been the biblical Kish.[38] He also suggested comparison with the name of the Arabic deity *qais* found in the tribal name *banû-qais* and the personal name '*abd 'al-qais*. We now know from Edomite personal names that Qaus was a deity worshipped in Edom, but whether we are to seek the origin of the name here or elsewhere cannot at present be determined.[39] At any rate, no Israelite derivation is known.

A relatively high percentage of the Saulite names are *hapax legomena*: Aphiah (1 Sam. ix.1), Zeror (id.), Matri (1 Sam. x.21, though cf. Matred; Gen. xxxvi.39), Merab and Michal (1 Sam. xiv.49). For an even greater number, about twelve, no Israelite origin is known.[40] Ner and Abner, both of which occur in the early sources and in the Chronicler's Saulite genealogy, present a special problem. Ner was discovered among the el-Jîb graffiti;[41] a circumstance which must strengthen the Gibeonite associations of Saul's family. It occurs both in a Hurrian text at Ras Shamra and in a personal name formed with the Hurrian '*wr* (=lord).[42] Its occurrence in the Aramaic treaty from Sefire is problematic but the context certainly suggests the name of a deity.[43] Other non-Israelite theophoric names among the Saulites are Ishbaal (2 Sam. ii.8 etc.),[44] Meribbaal (1 Chron. viii.34 cf. Mephibaal; 2 Sam. ix.2; xxi.8), Alemeth and Azmaveth (1 Chron. viii.36). Malchishua (1 Sam. xiv.49) contains the same theophoric element as Elishua (2 Sam. v.15; 1 Chron. xiv.5), Abishua (1 Chron. v.30f. etc.) and Bathshua (Gen. xxxviii.2, 12; 1 Chron. ii.3). We may suspect, but cannot prove, that this deity was worshipped among the Hurrians.[45] Palti, a name borne by the second husband of Michal, daughter of Saul (1 Sam. xxv.45), occurs among the Ḫabiru of Nuzi and is almost certainly Hurrian, as also is Aiah borne by the father of Rizpah one of Saul's concubines (2 Sam. iii.7; xxi.10).[46]

The traditions about Saul which have been allowed to survive do not permit us to reconstruct a clear picture of his origins. Neither his Benjaminite pedigree (1 Sam. ix.1f.) nor his emergence as 'judge' would oblige us to consider him at this stage a Yahwist any more than, for example, Shamgar ben-Anath or Jerubbaal or Abimelech. Indications of his connection with groups east of the Jordan are not lacking. As has just been seen, his own name and that of several of his family including, perhaps, that of his father, were not unknown in early Edom.[47] An Edomite, Doeg, was one of the most faithful and possibly one of the highest placed of his servants.[48] In view of the associations between Edomites and Kenites it is further significant that he did not proceed against the latter in his Amalekite campaign (1 Sam. xv.6).[49] The narrative of 1 Sam. xi.1ff. also seems to presuppose a treaty, this time with the people of Jabesh-gilead. It will be recalled that in the tribal coalition against Benjamin (Judges xx–xxi) the men of Jabesh-gilead were the only ones who did not contribute to the war of extermination (xxi.8f.), and the ensuing narrative seems to presuppose ethnic affinities between Gilead and Benjamin (verses 12–14). After the battle of Gilboa the Jabesh-gileadites rescued the mutilated bodies of Saul and his sons, cremated them in their own city and gave them temporary interment.[50] The reaction of David on hearing the news of what they had done (2 Sam. ii.4*b*–7) strengthens the impression that a definite treaty-relationship had existed between Saul and these people.[51] We may further note that Gilead is mentioned first of the territories under the rule of Ishbaal (2 Sam. ii.9) now established at Mahanaim.

In view of the proximity of Geshur and Maacah to Gilead it is worth noting that the genealogical lists of the Chronicler point to some ethnic affinity between Maacah and the Gibeonite population (1 Chron. viii.29; ix.35). Moreover, Geshurites are found in the Negeb (2 Sam. xvii.24–9) and the king of Geshur contemporary with David bears the same name as one of the non-Israelite and pre-Israelite groups around Hebron, a name which is very probably Hurrian.[52] We are clearly not in a position, in the present state of our knowledge, to interpret these many converging pieces of evidence satisfactorily. But they are consistent with the view that the Gibeonites belonged to a strain represented also in pre-monarchical Edom, the south of Judah and various locations across the Jordan, and that the origins of Saul and his family must also be sought here.[53]

With regard to Saul, this hypothesis would not be invalidated by the campaign which he waged against the Gibeonites any more than it would by the fact that he fought against Edom (1 Sam. xiv.47). 2 Sam. xxi.2 attributes his hostility towards the Gibeonites to his 'zeal', which may well be interpreted as the zeal of a recent convert to Yahwism – though of course purely political and strategical factors were also involved. In this respect the situation may not have been so different from that of Abimelech at Shechem. He too, despite ethnic ties (Judges ix.1–3), was soon involved in hostile action against the city.

As is well known, the redactional history behind the traditions in 1 Sam. is extremely complicated and the task of historical evaluation correspondingly difficult. Yet if we leave out of account such late and theologically coloured passages as vii.2–17,[54] a fairly clear sequence of events emerges with respect to Israelite–Philistine relations. After the battle of Aphek (1 Sam. iv.1*b*ff.) and the consequent capture of the ark and destruction of Shiloh (cf. Jer. vii.12; xxvi.6), the Philistines were able to control at least the Shephelah and Central Highlands, including the Gibeonite region. It is possible, as we have seen,[55] that they established a garrison or military command post in Gibeon in keeping with their general practice. Their purpose at this point seems to have been complete conquest of the country in which they had begun to settle about a century and a half earlier.[56] The successful military action referred to set them well on the way towards this goal; and we may suppose that for several years after this event there were several attempts to break their stranglehold (e.g. 1 Sam. xiii.2–7) or at least disrupt their programme of pacifying the occupied territories.[57] The situation at this time must have been very confused. We hear, for example, of 'Hebrews' (cf. the '*Apiru* of the Amarna letters) serving in the Philistine army, as David was later to do, and defecting to the Israelites after the successful *coup de main* of

Jonathan (xiv. 21). It is clear from xiii.3 (cf. iv.9) that these 'Hebrews', including the Israelites, were considered juridically subject to the Philistines.[58]

The successful action of Jonathan described in xiv led to a decisive set-back for the Philistines who retreated to the coastal plain (xiv.23) and were unable to launch any further attack until the end of the reign. Desultory fighting continued (xviii.27, 30; xxiii.1ff.), but their stranglehold was broken for the time being. We have good reason to believe that the Gibeonites, together with their Israelite confederates, had become subject to the Philistines though we have no means of determining exactly when this happened. After Saul's victory the Philistines were driven back west of the Gibeonite region (xiv.31). We learn later that the sword of the Philistine giant was deposited as an *ex-voto* in the Nob sanctuary (xxi.9) and Nob, according to the most probable identification, was little more than four air miles from Gibeon.[59] After the retreat of the Philistines to the coastal plain via Beth-horn (xiv.23),[60] Saul set up his first altar to Yahweh on 'the great stone' used for the sacrifice of the captured animals (verses 33, 35). As suggested earlier, this may well be identical with 'the great stone which is in Gibeon' (2 Sam. xx.8) and with the altar upon which Solomon offered sacrifices (1 Kings iii.4). The conclusion would at any rate appear inescapable that the ark, located in a Gibeonite city, was for the period following this victory accessible to Saul and the Israelites. This opens up new possibilities of interpreting the religious and cultic aspects of the reign of Saul.

What happened to Gibeon at this point of its history and how may we explain the antagonism of Saul towards its inhabitants? Various possibilities suggest themselves: that Saul for political reasons was determined to eliminate non-Israelite enclaves; that he was uncertain of its loyalty in the struggle with the Philistines which he knew was bound to continue; that the Gibeonites had already compromised themselves either by neutrality or active collusion with the enemy.[61] A further suggestion, original but by no means impossible, has been made, namely, that Saul at this time attempted to make Gibeon his capital, impressed as he must have been by its prestige as a religious centre, its impressive fortifications and hydraulic works and, not least, its commanding strategic position.[62] This hypothesis is strongly supported by the term *habbāmāh hagg$^{e}$d̲ôlāh* applied to Gibeon in 1 Kings iii.4 and the fact that Solomon went there rather than elsewhere for the inaugural revelation of his reign.[63] It is also intrinsically probable that it was at the Gibeonite sanctuary that David 'sought the face of Yahweh' before handing over the descendants of Saul to the Gibeonites (2 Sam. xxi.1).[64] Whether support for the hypothesis can be found in the results of excavation at el-Jîb is doubtful since no exact dating can be established.[65] But as far as the Old Testament tradition is concerned, there is nothing that contradicts and much that commends it; and it would, at the same time, be fully consonant with the Chronicler's association between Saul and Gibeon.

After the defeat and death of Saul (1 Sam. xxviii–xxxi) the Gibeonite region must have fallen once again under Philistine control. This is implied by 2 Sam. v.25 where we learn that the transfer of the ark to Jerusalem was made possible by the defeat of the Philistines 'from Gibeon[66] to Gezer'.

The cultic importance of Gibeon during the reign of Saul has been to a good extent obscured because of theological and polemical factors operating throughout the history of the tradition. It is, however, clearly attested in 1 Kings iii.4 (=2 Chron. i.3–6) and in further indications in the Chronicler's work and later Jewish writings. We may emphasize here a point made earlier, that the Gibeonite 'great high place' was, in all probability, the central sanctuary of the Gibeonite cities which formed an identifiable political–ethnic unity. A vital aspect of this importance, often overlooked, is that the ark was left in a Gibeonite city shortly before the accession of Saul and taken thence to Jerusalem not long after his death. This item of information given us by the historical tradition in 1–2 Sam. raises questions of evident significance for the religious history of Israel, and to these we now turn.

CHAPTER VI

# GIBEON AND THE ARK: A HYPOTHESIS

Having established in outline the history of the Philistine war during Saul's reign we pass on to the role played by the ark in this war, with special reference to the statement in 1 Sam. vii. 2 that it was lodged in a Gibeonite city. Since it was taken into battle against the Philistines (1 Sam. iv. 3ff.; 2 Sam. xi. 11), it is reasonable to regard it as a war-palladium and with it the title 'Yahweh of the hosts' was closely associated.[1] We questioned in the previous chapter the common assumption that it was simply neglected during the reign of Saul; and it is worthy of note that both Saul and David employed priests descended from the ark-priesthood of Shiloh.

Though taken into battle in particularly critical moments, the ark was generally housed in a sanctuary. At Shiloh it was in 'the house of Yahweh' (1 Sam. i. 7; iii. 15) and after its return from Philistine territory in 'the house of Abinadab on the hill' (1 Sam. vii. 1 [R.S.V.]). There is no record of its moving after this time until David brought it to Jerusalem.

In rabbinical tradition the three 'divine residences' before the building of the temple were Shiloh, Nob and Gibeon.[2] The selection of these three is clearly due to the belief that the Tent, and therefore the Shekinah, was located there. The Priestly writer places the Tent at Shiloh (Joshua xviii. 1) and the Chronicler at Gibeon (1 Chron. xvi. 39). Nob may have been added as a result of identifying the tent in which David placed the Philistine's armour (1 Sam. xvii. 54) with the priestly tent. According to the Priestly writer ark and tent were together. The Chronicler, for reasons which will be discussed later, locates the ark in Jerusalem and the tent in Gibeon during the early part of the reign of Solomon. Neither, however, mentions Nob; but there are indications in 1 Sam. xxi–xxii, which do not amount to proof, that this sanctuary may have been thought of as housing the ark.

(i) The Nob priesthood was descended from that of Shiloh which is associated with the ark. Saul's priest Ahijah would appear to be identical with Ahimelech priest of Nob since the father's name is the same for both.[3] Abiathar, son of Abimelech, became David's priest and remained in office until deposed by Solomon. His life was spared because he had been an ark-priest (1 Kings ii.26). The appointment of Abiathar by David is consonant with the latter's solicitude to bring the ark to Jerusalem and thus strengthen his claim to the religious allegiance of Israel. A further indication is that the slaughter of the Nob priesthood fulfils the prophetic oracle directed against the priesthood of Shiloh (1 Sam. ii.31–3; xxii.11ff.).

(ii) According to 1 Sam. xxi.5, the Nob sanctuary contained the 'bread of the presence'. Exod. xxv.23–30 speaks of this in a context dealing with the ark, with which may be compared Lev. xxiv.5ff. referring to the twelve loaves at the central sanctuary which clearly correspond to the twelve tribes. Although a late text, this last at least witnesses to an association between the ark at the central sanctuary and the holy bread. In this respect it may be significant that it was a prophet from Shiloh, Ahijah, who performed the dramatic gesture of tearing his cloak into twelve parts (1 Kings xi.29ff.).[4]

(iii) The placing of the giant Philistine's armour in the Nob sanctuary (1 Sam. xxi.9; cf. xxxi.10) and the presence of the ephod indicate at least the privileged status of this cult-centre. The need for ritual purification before eating the shewbread (xxi.4ff.) points in the same direction; and we recall that Uriah's refusal to sleep with his wife during the Ammonite campaign is motivated by the sacral nature of the war and the presence of the ark among the troops (2 Sam. xi.11). We have reason to believe that David's 'enquiring of God' at Nob (1 Sam. xxii.13) had something to do with the outcome of his struggle against Saul (cf. xxii.12ff.). The oracle is not mentioned in the account of David's visit to Nob, and it seems strange that there were not five loaves of bread in this 'city of priests' (xxii.19) of whom there were at least eighty-five with their wives and children (xxii.18f.). Perhaps behind this puzzling narrative there lies an action similar to that performed by Ahijah of Shiloh in his encounter with Jeroboam (1 Kings xi. 29–31) confirming David's eventual ascendancy over the tribes.

On the hypothesis that there was but one ark[5] and that Nob was for a time an ark-sanctuary, we would have to conclude that the ark was moved from the Gibeonite city where it lay to another site during this period.[6] Several scholars, however, have sought to obviate this necessity by supposing that the Nob of 1 Sam. xxi–xxii, unlike the locality referred to in Isa. x. 32 and Neh. xi. 32, is identical with the Gibeonite sanctuary.[7] Without necessarily accepting all the arguments advanced in support of this hypothesis we may at least give it our attention. We are not obliged to identify the place referred to in Isa. x. 32 and Neh. xi. 32 with the scene of the events recorded in 1 Sam. xxi–xxii. The word itself, in all probability, means 'hill' or 'mountain',[8] consonant with the place-name Nebo in Transjordan mentioned in the Old Testament and in the Moabite inscription.[9] It would therefore be appropriate as a designation for the Gibeonite cult-centre whether we situate this at Gibeon or on nearby Nebi Samwil. The assumption that the massacre of the Nob priesthood explains the reference to Saul's anti-Gibeonite activity in 2 Sam. xxi. 1ff. is probably exaggerated, but there may well be a connection. According to 1 Sam. xxii. 19 the entire population of Nob, not just the priests, was liquidated; and in view of the degeneration (from the pure Yahwist point of view) of the Shiloh cultus and its personnel,[10] it is not impossible that Saul, at the height of his short-lived enthusiasm for Yahwism, would have taken such an action. The cultic settlement destroyed by Saul and the Edomite Doeg certainly seems to have been of some importance: it is described as 'a city of priests' (1 Sam. xxii. 19) of whom there were at least eighty-six (verses 18, 20ff.). Finally, the function of Doeg is in some ways similar to that of the Gibeonites referred to in the account of the treaty.[11]

These arguments do not amount to proof. If, with the majority of commentators, we still prefer to locate the Nob of

1 Sam. xxi.1ff. near Gibeah of Saul then it seems to us that Saul must have transferred the ark from the Gibeonite city where it had been left to a site near Gibeah and that after his final defeat it would have been brought back there. In view of the arguments just advanced, however, it seems more probable that the vicissitudes of the ark during this obscure period are indissolubly linked with what happened between Saul and the Gibeonites, and that after his initial military success Saul attempted to make Gibeon the centre of his kingdom and to authenticate his rule from the religious point of view by means of the ark-sanctuary established there. In so doing he would have provided a valuable precedent for David, one of whose first actions was to found a new capital and legitimize his rule by establishing the ark in it.[12] This view can, however, be defended only after a careful analysis of the relevant historical traditions contained in 1–2 Sam. and a closer look at 1 Sam. vi.21 – vii.2 in particular.

The first question which comes up for consideration here is that of the many cult places mentioned in the texts covering the pre-monarchical and early monarchical periods. The view of Wellhausen, still widely accepted, that cult-centrality was not an ancient institution in Israel seems to be borne out by the great plurality of cult centres: Gilgal (1 Sam. x.8; xi.15), Mizpah (x.17), Ramah (viii.4; xv.34; xix.18ff.), Beersheba (viii.2), Bethel (x.3), Gibeah or 'the hill' (x.5, 10) and Nob (xxi–xxii).[13] Yet, as pointed out in different ways by Alt and Noth,[14] the existence of a central sanctuary (or perhaps more than one) does not rule out local cults and cult centres even for a period much later than that of Saul. An examination of the narratives about Gilgal and Shiloh in particular would suggest that the Deuteronomists were attempting to revive an ancient institution and that the ark was the centre of tribal worship in the pre-monarchic period.[15] At all events, with the passage to monarchy a new and decisive element entered into play and a central sanctuary became if not necessary at least highly desirable. The abortive attempt of Abimelech to found a dynasty began with a move from Ophrah to the ancient cult-centre of Shechem. David lost no time in founding a new capital and transporting thither the ark as the palladium of at least some of the tribes. Until a few years before the accession of Saul Shiloh was the ark-sanctuary and a place of tribal gathering; according to Joshua xviii. 1 and xix. 51 the division of tribal territory was carried out there.[16] Saul is anointed *nāgîḏ* after visiting an unnamed sanctuary (1 Sam. x. 1) though prophetic confirmation only came when he arrived at *giḇʿaṯ hāʾᵉlōhîm* (x. 5, 10). In xi. 15 he is made king at Gilgal and in x. 24, generally recognized as late, at Mizpah. Thus there appear to be at least four cultic centres in Benjamin (five, including Nob) involved in the early history of Saul's reign and no mention at all of Gibeon 'the great high place'.

In view of the prestige and importance of the central Gibeonite sanctuary it is not surprising that scholarly hypotheses have abounded in explanation of its role, if any, in the history of this period. Those who accept the substantial historicity of the Chronicler's cultic history of Israel tend to give it considerable significance.[17] An important aspect of this problem is the identification of the 'place' where some Gibeonites were assigned to serve as 'hewers of wood and drawers of water' (Joshua ix. 23, 27). For the Deuteronomist editor this was certainly Jerusalem (cf. Deut. xii. 5) and the later tradition associating the *nethinim* with the Gibeonites is consonant with this. But Jerusalem could not have been the original place; the most obvious inference is that this was the Gibeonite sanctuary itself, especially in view of the cultic associations between Gibeon and Jerusalem which were discussed earlier.[18] The obscure oracle on Benjamin in Deut. xxxiii. 12 also seems to refer indirectly to a Benjaminite sanctuary since it refers twice to a deity 'dwelling' (*škn*) within the boundaries of that tribe.[19] If we date it in the eleventh or early tenth century the original reference, once again, can hardly have been to Jerusalem and *may* have been to the important Gibeonite sanctuary.[20] At all events, the problem of the many Benjaminite sanctuaries at this time remains.

This brings us back to the basic issue of centrality of cult in the pre-monarchical period and the reign of Saul. Wellhausen's thesis was soon challenged by a number of scholars. Schlatter, perplexed by the absence of any reference to Nebi Samwil which appeared to be the most favoured site for a great religious centre in Benjamin, concluded that Gibeon, Mizpah, Gibeah of God and Nob are all roughly synonymous terms designating the one central Benjaminite sanctuary at Nebi Samwil.[21] Van Hoonacker argued that cult centrality goes back beyond Deuteronomy to Moses and his thesis was developed by his pupil H. A. Poels with respect to the traditions in 1 Sam.[22] Poels took the drastic expedient of assuming that Gilgal, Gibeah, Mizpah and Nob are not proper names at all but different designations of the one central sanctuary located at Nebi Samwil. *haggiḇʿāh* of 1 Sam. vii. 1 and 2 Sam. vi. 3, though apparently situated at Kiriath-jearim, refers to the same place since the people of Kiriath-jearim and Gibeon shared the same sanctuary which was situated between the two cities.

The radical solution of Poels did not win over adherents then and it has not since.[23] The chief defects of his study were his cavalier treatment of Palestinian topography and his failure to test his theory against a careful study of the traditions in 1 Sam. Notwithstanding the negative critical verdict on Poels's work we find the same 'paradoxe topographique'[24] reappearing in a later work of A. Bruno who also identified Saul's hostile action against the Gibeonites with the slaughter of the Nob priesthood.[25] The same tendency towards topographical assimilation appeared in a briefer study of Hertzberg on Mizpah who, while criticizing Bruno, reproduced a number of his conclusions.[26]

One difficulty which several of these authors feel and attempt to solve is why the ark should have been left at Kiriath-jearim rather than at Gibeon, obviously the most important of the four cities. Kosters had already suggested that Kiriath-jearim may have been considered a convenient place to leave the ark for the brief period between David's victory and the capture of Jerusalem. For him the whole account in 1 Sam. vi is fictitious; in reality the Philistines kept the ark at their own city of Gath where it remained until their defeat recorded in 2 Sam. v.22–5.[27] This view can be ruled out for several reasons, principally its gratuitous assumption that 1 Sam. vi is unhistorical and that the city of Obed-edom the Gittite is identical with Philistine Gath. Brinker reproduced Poels's view that Kiriath-jearim and Gibeon shared the one sanctuary of Nebi Samwil and identified Nob as the section of this religious centre reserved for the priests.[28] We may finally recall once again van den Born's identification of the Gibeah of Judges xix–xx with Gibeon and his interpretation of this narrative as dealing indirectly with Saul's attempt to destroy the Gibeonites.[29]

To have a reasonable chance of acceptance any solution of the problem attacked by these authors must presuppose a careful examination of the narratives in 1–2 Sam. which inform us on the ark during this period. 1 Sam. i–iii deals for the most part with Samuel, and the ark is mentioned only incidentally (iii.3). iv.1*b* – vii.1, on the contrary, has the vicissitudes of the ark as its central theme and must be considered a separate source attached editorially to i–iii.[30] Earlier commentators were inclined to assign sources in 1 Sam. to J and E as in the Pentateuch; in particular, passages dealing with the ark were often allotted to E.[31] Confidence in this method declined sharply after the appearance of Rost's important study of the Davidic Succession History[32] and this rigid application of a documentary theory in Samuel is no longer in favour today.

In the work alluded to Rost contended that a separate ark-source, distinct from and introductory to the Davidic Succession History, came into existence in Jerusalem during the United Monarchy and is extant in the Old Testament in 1 Sam. iv.1*b* – vii.1 and 2 Sam. vi.[33] It may be described as the *hieros logos* of the new Jerusalemite sanctuary and formed part of the theological justification and authentication of the new dynasty. Rost further suggested that the narratives in 1–2 Sam. may represent only part of such an ark-narrative but unfortunately did not go on to discuss the possibility tha a section of such a hypothetical narrative, dealing with the sojourn of the ark in a Gibeonite city before the time of David, had been omitted. Our whole problem is to know what happened between 1 Sam. vii. 1 and 2 Sam. vi. 1.

Difficulties have been raised against this hypothesis of a continuous ark-source from different directions. Some have felt that 1 Sam. iv. 1*b*ff. belonged more to legend than to history,[34] while others prefer to read 2 Sam. vi as part of a larger David narrative-cycle.[35] The well known differences between the end of the first narrative and the beginning of the second have persuaded others again that there is no real connection between the two at all.[36] This last certainly seems to be exaggerated. The stations of the ark in Philistine territory end with it in the house of Abinadab and 2 Sam. vi begins at this point. Moreover, in both narratives the ark is placed in a new cart drawn, respectively, by two cows and the two sons of the priest (1 Sam. vi. 7; 2 Sam. vi. 3). The Perez-uzzah episode in 2 Sam. vi. 6ff. is paralleled by the cultic sin and chastisement of the Beth-shemeshites in 1 Sam. vi. 19 and in both references to a place-name there is *lusus verborum*.[37] David's question (2 Sam. vi. 9) is similar to that of the Beth-shemeshites (1 Sam. vi. 20). Rejoicing accompanies the presence of the ark in both narratives (1 Sam. vi. 13; 2 Sam. vi. 12) and the proceedings are crowned with a sacrifice in both cases (1 Sam. vi. 4; 2 Sam. vi. 13). The duration of the ark's exile among the Philistines is noted in 1 Sam. vi. 1 and that of its sojourn in the house of Obed-edom in 2 Sam. vi. 11. The bringing up of the ark to Jerusalem is the outcome of a military victory (2 Sam. vi. 1 following v. 25) as its loss was the outcome of a defeat.

It may, in addition, be tentatively suggested that a reading of the two sections consecutively reveals a certain structural and thematic pattern. Initially the ark was at Shiloh in 'the house of Yahweh' (iii. 7). There follow three stations in Philistine territory: Ashdod ('the house of Dagon', v. 2), Gath and Ekron despite the fact that *five* Philistine cities are mentioned in the first part of the narrative (vi. 17). After the Philistines give it up there are again three stations: Beth-shemesh ('the house [temple] of ŠMŠ'), Kiriath-jearim ('the house of Abinadab', vii. 1) and Gittaim ('the house of Obed-edom', 2 Sam. vi. 10). Finally it is set up in Jerusalem ('*the* house', 2 Sam. vii. 5, etc.). A glance at the locations between Shiloh and Jerusalem will reveal how ambiguous, from the Yahwist viewpoint, was the cult associated with the ark during this period.

The view that 1 Sam. iv. 1*b* – vii. 1 is pure legend is surely arbitrary. Many stories must have been in circulation about the ark before its permanent establishment in Jerusalem all of which may well have been embellished by legendary elements. The motivation for preserving those which spoke of the discomforting of the Philistines is obvious, but it is quite possible that stories of equal length about the later phases of its history were in circulation. As will be seen, 1 Sam. vi. 18*b*–19 represents a conflation of two accounts of what happened after the ark arrived in Beth-shemesh and 2 Sam. vi. 11 looks like a brief summary of a longer tradition or narrative about the three-month sojourn of the ark in the house of Obed-edom the Gittite. The differences between 1 Sam. iv. 1*b*ff. and 2 Sam. vi. 1–19 are surely to be explained with reference to the cultic aspects of the latter; as is clear by comparison with Pss. cxxxii and xxiv, what is described here is a procession ending in the Jerusalem sanctuary.[38] This is supported by indications in the narrative itself: the solemn proemium (verse 2), the exalted title of the ark (verse 2*b*; cf. Ps. xxiv. 10), the question of David (verse 9) answered in the liturgy of Ps. xxiv (verses 4–5), the solemnity and awe, the sacrifices and sacred dancing, and, not least, the reference to 'the fields of Jaar' in Ps. cxxxii. 6.[39]

Some of the arguments adduced in favour of direct continuity between 2 Sam. v. 17–25 and vi. 1–19 as parts of a 'David source' are far from convincing. Since the opening *wayyōsep* of the latter passage must be emended with LXX to *wayye'ᵉsōp* it does not correspond with the opening *wayyōsīpû* of

v. 22. The adverb *'ôḏ* (vi. 1; cf. v. 22) would suggest that vi. 2ff. has been editorially linked with the preceding narrative by representing the ark's return as the outcome of a culminating victory. The Baal-perazim episode in v. 20 is not parallel with Perez-uzzah (vi. 6–8) which, as we have seen, comes much closer to the chastisement of the Beth-shemeshites in the first narrative. In any case, the play on the word *perez* is found elsewhere in the Old Testament (Gen. xxxviii. 29; cf. Exod. xix. 22, 24). Even less convincing is the simple recurrence of *ṣā'aḏ* (vi. 13; cf. v. 24).[40]

The conclusion suggests itself, therefore, that a connection does exist between the ark-narratives in 1 and 2 Sam. The parallels and similarities adduced do not lead necessarily to the conclusion that the two passages belonged to a continuous ark-narrative but they are consistent with such a hypothesis.[41] If anything was known about the ark and its vicissitudes during the period on which the tradition is silent nothing of this has survived; and this may well be due to the conscious choice of those Jerusalem circles to whom we owe the present form of the ark narrative in 2 Sam. vi.

We now turn to the last few verses of the first narrative (1 Sam. vi. 18*b* – vii. 1). After seven months among the Philistines (vi. 1) the decision is made to return the ark (vi. 2). Beth-shemesh is evidently chosen as the nearest point outside the Philistine region and is considered to be Israelite ('its own land', vi. 9). We are not told how long the ark remained at Beth-shemesh; but some misfortune overtook its inhabitants which was attributed to the presence of the ark. As all the commentators agree, vi. 18*b*–19 is very corrupt and any attempt to reconstruct the original text must be to some extent conjectural. Reading *'d* as a substantive ('witness') rather than a preposition, verse 18*b* may be translated as follows: 'the great stone . . . is a witness to this day in the field of Joshua the Beth-shemeshite'.[42] It is not, however, clear to what the stone is meant to witness since no treaty has been mentioned. Tur-Sinai ingeniously suggested that behind the confusing text of verse 18*b* there lies an aetiological narrative about a place called Abel the Great (='great mourning') similar to Gen. 1.10f. (Abel-Mizraim).[43] Despite the difficulty against this view of the *'eben gᵉdôlāh* of verse 14 and the need to excise *'ālēhā* it may certainly be considered especially in view of the verb *'ābal* occurring in the following verse and the fact that the *mᵉnûḥāh* of the ark is always a place, a sanctuary, never a stone. We would therefore have a conflation of two traditions: the first, of a great mourning occasioned by the fifty thousand casualties mentioned in verse 19 and following inexplicably after 'seventy men'; the second, recording the death of seventy men as a result of looking at (into?) the ark.[44] LXX explains the disaster as punishment for hostility towards, or at least lack of enthusiasm for, the ark on the part of the sons of Jeconiah.[45] We are not told who these sons of Jeconiah were, but the name is of a type frequently found among Levites.[46] We would thus have an interesting parallelism between the situation in Beth-shemesh and in the Gibeonite cities since Uzzah son of Abinadab also has a Levitical name and the circumstances of his death provide an aetiological explanation of a place-name (2 Sam. vi.6–8).[47]

We should pause briefly here to note the interesting indications scattered throughout the Old Testament of association between Beth-shemesh and Gibeon with its cities. Beth-shemesh occurs in the list of Judahite boundary points together with Ekron and Kiriath-jearim (Joshua xv.10) and is found, again with Ekron, in the Danite city-list (Joshua xix.41).[48] Together with other Danite cities, Beth-shemesh formed the second administrative district of Solomon (1 Kings iv.9), and this is in conformity with the Danite list in Joshua xix which also goes back, in all probability, to the early monarchical period.[49] This is further confirmed by the occurrence of Beth-shemesh among the Levitical cities (Joshua xxi.16; cf. 1 Chron. vi.44 M.T.) since these lists also come from the same period.[50]

Judges i.34f. provides valuable information on the non-Israelite ('Amorite') element in the territory of Dan in the early period. It seems reasonable to suppose that the failure of this tribe to assimilate or contain this element was responsible, together with Philistine pressure from the outside, for the migration of the Danites to the north. We do not know when the migration took place, but it is worth noting that immediately upon arrival they set up Micah's graven image, and that this was a good time before the destruction of Shiloh.[51] Despite uncertainties of interpretation, the archaeological evidence from Beth-shemesh (Tell er-Rumeileh near Ain Shems) would suggest that it was under Philistine control at least intermittently during the reign of Saul and did not become Israelite at least until the time of David.[52] This would make it easier for us to understand why the Philistines were willing to leave the potentially dangerous palladium in that city for so long as it remained under their control.

What we detect behind the confused traditions preserved in 1 Sam. vi. 14–21 is a definite stage of the ark's history, though one of unknown duration, comparable to the equally obscure period which followed after the ark was taken over by the inhabitants of Kiriath-jearim. Religious ideas and practices which must have been suspect from the Israelite viewpoint are attested for both Dan and Beth-shemesh on the one hand and Benjamin and the Gibeonite cities on the other. For the former we have the idol in the house of Micah (Judges xvii–xviii), the Samson cycle of stories, place-names with -ŠMŠ and the tradition behind 1 Sam. vi. 18*b*–19; for the latter, the *pᵉsîlîm* of Judges iii. 19, the crime of the men of Gibeah (Judges xix), the ritual immolation of the Saulites (2 Sam. xxi. 1–14) and other indirect indications.[53] Other interesting parallels between the situation in the two localities may be pointed out. The Danite sanctuary after the migration is served by a priesthood descended from Levi through Gershom son of Moses (Judges xviii. 30f.).[54] It was indicated earlier that the personal names associated with the ark during its stay in a Gibeonite city are of a kind found among the Levites (Eleazar is son of Aaron as Gershom is son of Moses) and that both Beth-shemesh and Gibeon were Levitical cities. Judges xviii. 30f. states that the Danite sanctuary remained in existence 'as long as the house of God was at Shiloh' and that the Danite priesthood lasted 'until the day of the exile of the land'. This last phrase is rather incongruous; we read of Israel, Judah, Jerusalem, Gilgal being exiled *from* the land,[55] but never, apart from this text, of the land itself being exiled. In view of the reference to the ark, recently at Shiloh, being exiled (1 Sam. iv. 21f.) an emendation from *hā'āreṣ* to *hā'ᵃrôn* commends itself. This would give added weight to the importance of the ark during the period in question.

According to Judges xviii. 2 the Danites camped at Kiriath-jearim, a site later known as 'the camp of Dan', on their movement northwards. In this migration the clans of Zora and Eshtaol played a significant role (Judges xviii. 2, 11), and according to the Chronicler (1 Chron. iv. 2; ii. 53) these are ethnically related to people settled in Kiriath-jearim. Uncertain of interpretation as these data are, we may take them to be further indications of association during this early period between elements of the population of the two tribal regions of Dan and Benjamin.

Pursuing our investigation of the end of the ark-narrative in 1 Sam. iv. 1*b* – vii. 1, we should note that the removal of the ark from Beth-shemesh did not involve, as is commonly supposed, a passage from one Israelite city to another. As we have seen, Beth-shemesh was at this time a non-Israelite city under Philistine control and Kiriath-jearim was Gibeonite. That the message was sent to the people of Kiriath-jearim is understandable since the latter was only eight miles distant and the nearest point to Beth-shemesh in the Judah boundary-list (Joshua xv. 9f.). This, however, may not be the entire explanation in view of what was said in the previous paragraph. If, moreover, the biblical Rabbah (*rbt* in the Thutmoses III list) may be identified with Beth-shemesh the connection between the two cities emerges even more clearly since Kiriath-jearim and Rabbah form one separate unit in the Judah city-list (Joshua xv. 60).[56]

The people of Kiriath-jearim took the ark from their neighbours, and of its new location we are told *in this source* only two particulars which are repeated at the beginning of the second narrative (2 Sam. vi.3): that they brought it to the house of Abinadab; that this house was *baggiḇʿāh*. It may seem logical to infer, what is stated explicitly in the separate source which follows (vii.2), that this location is in Kiriath-jearim; but in fact this is not stated explicitly and the request addressed to the people of Kiriath-jearim to 'take it up to you' could refer to them *qua* Gibeonites.

For the hypothesis presented here it is crucial to note that a new source begins with 1 Sam. vii.2. Here we find recorded the passing of twenty years after which Samuel convoked a plenary gathering of the tribes similar to that presided over by Joshua at Shechem (Joshua xxiv). As we noted earlier, the number of years – awkwardly and parenthetically interposed between the subordinate and main clauses – follows the pattern of the Deuteronomic editor of the book of Judges, which in its turn would lead us to think of the homily and battle taking place after that period of time.[57] The homily is clearly Deuteronomic in style and theme; indeed, the whole passage (verses 2–17) is in accord with Deuteronomic thinking.[58] The location of the episode at Mizpah recalls the most recent narrative-strand in Judges xx–xxi and looks forward to 1 Sam. x.17–27 and xii, all of which passages bear clear marks of Deuteronomic editing.[59] It was intimated in an earlier chapter that this narrative cannot be used with any confidence as historical source material, especially with regard to the time-span indicated.[60] Without going so far as to characterize it as legendary,[61] none of the information which it provides can be taken at face value, and this would also be true of the statement found near the beginning concerning the location of the ark during this period.

Having made this point clearly, however, we must go on to note the possibility, indeed probability, that the editors had access to earlier sources nearer to the time of the events described.[62] We are told that this was the time when Israel 'lamented after Yahweh' (vii.2). The verb *nāhāh* elsewhere connotes a ritual lamentation for the dead (cf. Mic. ii.4; Ezek. xxxii.18), thus suggesting a lamentation for the 'exiled' ark (cf. 'the glory has departed from Israel', iv.21f.). We have seen that this 'exile' would have ended temporarily with Saul's victory (1 Sam. xiv), and it is of interest to note that the present narrative contains a description of a Philistine defeat brought about by the miraculous intervention of Yahweh (verses 7–13*a*), one which has several significant points in common with the account of a later Philistine defeat at the hands of David resulting in the rescue of the ark (2 Sam. v.17–25).[63] In view of all this, it would be reasonable to suggest that we have here, beneath the polemical re-editing, an account of a victory won not by Samuel but by Saul. The reference to the 'foreign gods' (verse 3) could then be seen to refer to the suspect religious practices and cult of the Gibeonites among whom the ark had resided during this period just as the 'foreign gods' of Gen. xxxv.2 and Joshua xxiv.23 refer to those of Shechem. Finally, we may note that in 1–2 Sam. the term 'Amorite' is found only here (verse 14*b*) and in 2 Sam. xxi.2 where it refers to the Gibeonites. Hence the former reference could well be to the conclusion of hostilities between Saul and the Gibeonites the evidence for which we have already examined.

Before we can go on to examine more closely the crucial question of the location of the ark (vii.1), we need to raise some questions about the later narrative in 2 Sam. vi.1–19. It is preceded by the account of a double defeat of the Philistines by David (2 Sam. v.17–25). Literary and stylistic analysis suggest that these episodes form part of a loosely connected series of Philistine war stories,[64] and it is particularly noteworthy that the account of David's victories is resumed in viii.1 suggesting that vi–vii have been edited into the narrative at a definite and important stage of redaction. Moreover, of all these warlike episodes only v.17–25 contains a miraculous and theophanic element, similar to that in 1 Sam. vii.7–13*a*, and like this latter not unconnected with the ark.[65]

The most obvious link between 2 Sam. v.25 and vi.1ff. is topographical: the Philistines are defeated from Gibeon[66] to Gezer and the ark is removed from the Gibeonite city where it had been left. Moreover, the valley of Rephaim and Baal-perazim contain topographical elements elsewhere associated with the Gibeonite cities.[67] The narrative of the transference of the ark is introduced twice (verses 1–2). The first introduction evidently presupposes a military campaign: the numbers involved (30,000), the term *baḥûr*, the introductory adverb *'ôḏ* make this quite clear.[68] The difficulty is, of course, that what follows is not a military campaign at all. It must therefore be concluded that verse 1 is an editorial link with the preceding narrative showing how the ark was rescued as a result of a military victory.

This brings us to 2 Sam. vi.2, which we must take to be the original introduction to the narrative. It will not be necessary here to discuss exhaustively all the difficulties with which this verse bristles.[69] 1 Chron. xiii.6 has presumably interpreted *ba'ᵃlê yᵉhûḏāh* as a place-name referring to Kiriath-jearim, but since this leaves the preposition unexplained it seems methodologically sounder to retain the M.T. and interpret the word, with LXX$^B$ and Vulg., as 'free citizens' or 'rulers'.[70] A further difficulty is *miššām* which seems to call for an antecedent place-name. If, however, verse 1 is an editorial addition, it could refer back to v.25, the region cleared of the Philistines and Gibeon in particular. At this point the location of the ark is described once again as 'the house of Abinadab (which was) on the hill'. Disarmingly straightforward as it may seem, this description is not free of difficulties. Leaving aside the question whether 'house' refers to a private dwelling or a temple,[71] the names of the cultic functionaries associated with the ark in 1 Sam. vii.1 are suspiciously similar to the names of the well known sons of Aaron.[72] It may also not be out of place to note that the name Abinadab occurs in the Davidic genealogy – one of several indications linking David's family with an ethnic group settled in or near Kiriath-jearim.[73] In 2 Sam. vi.2ff. Eleazar is no longer mentioned and the ark is now in the charge of two other sons of Abinadab, Uzzah and Ahio (or possibly Uzzah and his brother), which may seem strange in view of the length of time separating the two important phases of the ark's history.

If *baggiḇʿāh* is taken to refer to the high place of Kiriath-jearim[74] it may be asked why such a relatively rare word is used instead of the more common *bāmāh* (cf. 1 Sam. ix. 12ff.). More difficult still is the location of the ark at a relatively insignificant place rather than at the important sanctuary of Gibeon, especially in view of the strong probability that the Gibeonite cities, as a definite political unit, would have had their own central sanctuary. In view of the secondary nature of 2 Sam. vi. 1 the mention of *haggiḇʿāh* without further specification as the location of the ark (verse 3) recalls at once for the hearer *giḇʿôn* mentioned in v. 25. Worthy of note is the fact that this word *giḇʿāh* occurs only four times in early historical narratives in the Old Testament and of these occurrences one, and possibly more than one, are associated with Gibeon.[75] It is quite clear, at any rate, that in 2 Sam. vi. 2 a special and well known hill is referred to, and in a way which invites comparison with 'the mountain (of Yahweh)' in 2 Sam. xxi. 6, 9, an expression which certainly refers to Gibeon and is also of rare occurrence.[76] We may recall once again that in 1 Kings iii. 4 Gibeon is the *bāmāh* par excellence, and as such it must have been widely known. It may also be significant in this respect that whereas Gibeon is a Levitical city Kiriath-jearim is not.

It must be emphasized that we are not pretending, and in view of the material at our disposal could not pretend, to prove that the ark was located at Gibeon or nearby Nebi Samwil before its transfer to Jerusalem. There are indications which, however, in our view, strongly suggest this conclusion especially on account of the Jerusalemite origin of 2 Sam. vi. 1–19 and the political and religious imperatives arising out of the new cultic situation in David's reign. We must remember that right into Solomon's reign Gibeon was the principal rival to the new cult-centre in Jerusalem.[77]

Granted this hypothesis, how did the tradition of a twenty-year sojourn of the ark at Kiriath-jearim arise? This tradition is attested only in the late and historically untrustworthy 1 Sam. vii. 2–17; 1 Chron. xiii. 5–6, depending on the Mizpah tradition at this point,[78] and probably Ps. cxxxii.6 referring to the discovery of the ark 'in the fields of Jaar' (cf. the ark in the field of Joshua, 1 Sam. vi.14). In its present form the first of these comes from the Deuteronomist historian while the other two are clearly traceable to Jerusalemite sources much concerned with the temple cult. In view of these origins, and in view also of the tendentious rewriting of early traditions by Judahite and Deuteronomist historians – a particularly clear case of which is 1 Kings xii[79] – it seems reasonable to suppose that the same process is involved here. Seen in this context, the fact that Kiriath-jearim is the only Gibeonite city ascribed to Judah (Joshua xv.60) and the only one with ethnic associations in Judahite territory[80] assumes a new significance. Furthermore, the earliest references to Levites in Old Testament historical tradition associate them with Judah and, more particularly, with Bethlehem (Judges xvii.7ff.; xix.1); and 2 Sam. xv.24 suggests that during David's reign the Levites were considered the legitimate bearers and guardians of the ark. That the names of cultic functionaries connected with the ark in the final phase of its history before its transfer to Jerusalem are Levitical may therefore reflect an attempt to legitimize David's action from the point of view of Jerusalemite 'orthodoxy'. 1 Kings iii.3–4 (cf. xiii.33) reveals quite clearly the Deuteronomist attitude to Gibeon, *habbāmāh haggᵉḏôlāh*. Though David himself was partial to the Gibeonites when they provided him with a convenient means for eliminating potential rivals (2 Sam. xxi.1–14), he and his successor could hardly have remained indifferent to the Gibeonite cult-centre as a strong potential rival to the new royal sanctuary in Jerusalem. 2 Sam. vi.1–19 makes it clear that the ark-God settled only where he chose to settle. It would certainly have been in the interests of the new cult-centre in Jerusalem to conceal or make little of the fact that his prior choice had been among the Gibeonites.

Such a reading of the history does not exclude the possibility that the men of Kiriath-jearim played a significant role with respect to the ark during this obscure period. This may be due to their situation astride the boundaries of Benjamin, Judah and Dan; at any rate, 1 Sam. vi.21 – vii.1 assigns to them the decisive role in the *procession* of the ark from Beth-shemesh to its new sanctuary 'on the hill'.[81] The same may be suggested by the reference to the finding of the ark in the fields of Jaar (Ps. cxxxii.6) though here the issue is confused, probably beyond hope of solution, by the parallelism of this place-name with Ephrathah.[82]

CHAPTER VII

# GIBEON DURING THE REIGNS OF DAVID AND SOLOMON

The successive stages in David's ascent to kingship over all Israel are fairly clearly delineated in the tradition. Renown in early life as a warrior earned him entry into Saul's service (1 Sam. xvi. 14–23; xvii. 55–8) and thereafter his courage and resource as a *condottiere* became even more widely known to the point of arousing the king's jealousy. We cannot say for certain at what point David conceived the ambition of succeeding to the kingship of Saul; but soon enough he was engaged in a running battle with Saul's forces during which he became in effect a vassal and ally of the Philistines.[1] After Saul's defeat and death he persuaded Judah and its associated tribes to anoint him king (2 Sam. ii. 1–4) after he had moved from Ziklag to the ancient cult-centre of Hebron-Mamre. Overtures with Jabesh-gilead, designed to renew the relationship which had existed under Saul, showed that David's ambitions were not confined to the south.[2] While Ishbaal's claim to succeed to the kingship was apparently widely recognized, the spectacular defeat of his father and the remoteness of Mahanaim considerably weakened his chances of establishing any effective rule. The expedition from Mahanaim to Gibeon, clearly the beginning of a major attempt to reassert Ishbaal's rule, ended in failure (2 Sam. ii. 12–17) and the Saulites were worsted in the ensuing hostilities which went on for some time (iii. 1). The defection of Abner sealed Ishbaal's fate and the assassination of both left no major obstacle in David's path. His kingship over the northern tribes, including Benjamin,[3] was ratified by covenant at Hebron (2 Sam. v. 1–3).

If we are to accept as even approximately correct the duration of thirty years for David's reign in Jerusalem (v. 5) the city must have been taken at an early date, though we cannot be certain that 2 Sam. v. 6ff. represents the original chronological sequence.[4] Once the city was in his hands, however, he wasted no time in establishing the ark-shrine in it with a view to strengthening the allegiance of Benjamin and its northern neighbours where Saul's appeal had been strongest.

There is some evidence that during this early period David had considerable support from Benjaminites and Gibeonites. He was sympathetically received by prophetic groups in Benjaminite Ramah (1 Sam. xix. 18ff.) and the account of his visit to the Nob sanctuary suggests that the priesthood also gave active support to his political claims.[5] The list of his warriors in 2 Sam. xxiii. 8ff. contains at least three names from Benjamin (Abiezer of Anathoth, Ittai of Gibeah, Azmaweth of Bahurim) as well as Naharai of Beeroth and two Ithrites who, according to the Chronicler (1 Chron. ii. 53), belonged to clans of Kiriath-jearim. The Chronicler has also left us a list of Benjaminites who defected from Saul and joined David at Ziklag, including a certain Ishmaiah, a prominent Gibeonite (1 Chron. xii. 1–7).[6] His acquiescence in the Gibeonite claim against Saul's family (2 Sam. xxi. 1–14) would indicate that he favoured some degree of autonomy for such ethnic enclaves and would not be contradicted by his execution of the two Beerothites who assassinated Ishbaal since this was dictated by political necessity. It would, in any case, be quite false to represent David as Israelite and Yahwist *tout court* over against ethnically and religiously alien groups such as the Gibeonites. According to what evidence has survived, his family was closely connected with Kenite and Kenizzite elements in the south, contained a strong Moabitic element and may even, as we saw earlier, have had some ethnic relationship with groups settled at an early date in or near Kiriath-jearim.[7] To judge by onomastic evidence, admittedly not in itself decisive, its adhesion to Yahwism was tenuous to say the least. Neither his father, nor he himself, nor any of his brothers has a Yahwist name. Of the sons born to him while at Hebron only two – Adonijah and Shephatiah – have such names and there is not a single one among the many offspring whom he begot after settling in Jerusalem.[8] He seems to have had little scruple in adopting Canaanite cultic practices, and the genuine and sometimes disconcerting piety which he evinces throughout does not necessarily derive from Yahwist inspiration.

Though indications are not abundant, we may be quite sure that Gibeon continued to be an important political and religious centre throughout his reign. Two important and fateful encounters took place there: between Abner and Joab (2 Sam. ii.12–17) and between the latter and Amasa (xx.8–10*a*). From these and other indications it seems that Gibeon was considered an important meeting place both then and later.[9] The expedition of Abner's forces from Mahanaim seems to have had the purpose of establishing Ishbaal's effective rule over the whole kingdom including the southern clans.[10] The most probable explanation of the 'playing' of the young men (ii.14) is that both sides agreed to parley (they *sat down* on either side of the pool) and that, as a result of their negotiations, they decided to settle the issue by a trial of arms between twelve warriors chosen from each side.[11] The issue being undecided – all twenty-four were killed – no alternative remained but all-out war.

It is important to note that the encounter at Gibeon was not by chance; the destination of the march was decided from the time they set out (ii.12, *giḇʿônāh*). This may strengthen the probability that Abner hoped to solve the impasse by negotiation, and in fact it was he who took the initiative after this second battle of Gibeon to arrange a truce (ii.26–8) and who later went to Hebron to negotiate David's rule over the northern tribes (iii.12ff.). Not surprisingly, Benjaminites played an important role in the Gibeon expedition (ii.15) and in the negotiations of Abner prior to the Hebron mission – it is clear that in this case Abner conferred with them separately (iii.19). This would seem to give added probability to the hypothesis of Gibeon as a royal capital during the latter part of the reign of Saul.[12]

The question where exactly the single combat and ensuing battle took place is of lesser importance and incapable of final solution but may be mentioned nonetheless. The initial meeting took place *'al bᵉrēkaṯ giḇ'ôn* (ii.13). Pritchard identifies this 'pool' with the great cylindrical cistern cleared during the excavations of 1956–7, which would imply that the meeting took place within the city limits.[13] While this is certainly possible, the location of the ensuing combat is later described as *ḥelqaṯ haṣṣūrîm 'ᵃšer bᵉgiḇ'ôn* in M.T. (v.16) which would more easily suggest an open space outside the city walls. An added difficulty is that we would naturally suppose the Philistines to have re-occupied the Central Highlands, including the Gibeonite region, after the decisive battle of Gilboa. While they could have had little objection to Israelites fighting among themselves and killing each other, the absence of any reference to them in the account of this expedition is somewhat disconcerting. For if Ishbaal and Abner had prevailed rather than David and Joab they would very soon have had to come to terms with a confident enemy greatly strengthened by its recent successes. In fact, we are told that they took action as soon as they heard that David had become king over Israel (v.17). It is, of course, not out of the question that the Gibeonites had on their own account established some form of *modus vivendi* with the Philistines and succeeded in maintaining a measure of neutrality in the Philistine–Israelite struggle.[14]

The location of the parley at sunset cannot be further determined since ii.24 provides no easy clues and may be corrupt. Nowhere else do we find any reference either to the hill of Ammah or Giah or the wilderness of Gibeon. However, the meaning 'aqueduct', 'canal', 'pipeline' is attested in post-biblical Hebrew for *'ammāh* and *gîaḥ* may mean 'spring of water' (cf. *gîḥôn*); hence it may be suggested that these are not proper names.[15] Since *miḏbar* may simply refer to grazing land there is no need to emend *giḇ'ôn* to *geḇa'*.

The second encounter at Gibeon, which ended with the treacherous assassination of Amasa by Joab (2 Sam. xx.8–10), would also seem not to have taken place at this great centre by mere accident. The occasion was another serious challenge to David's rule over the tribes instigated by Sheba ben-Bichri a Benjaminite and supported, it would seem, by the mass of the northern tribes ('all the men of Israel withdrew from David and followed Sheba ben-Bichri', verse 2). Since David was already at Gilgal (xix.40) it would appear reasonable to suggest that the secession was solemnly proclaimed from another Benjaminite religious centre, in which case Gibeon would be the chief contender especially since it was there that Amasa, obviously suspected of disaffection towards David, was found (xx.8). We have no further indication of the identity and whereabouts of 'the great stone which is in Gibeon' but comparison with the great stone which was in the field of Joshua at Beth-shemesh (1 Sam. vi.14 and perhaps 18) may be suggested since it was there that an ark-sanctuary was set up for a time. It is within the bounds of critical probability to suggest that here too we have a clue to the location of the ark-sanctuary during a good part of the reign of Saul. The name Sheba, moreover, is always accompanied by the gentilic *bkry* practically identical with *bkrt* and *bkrw* occurring in Saulite genealogies elsewhere (1 Sam. ix.1; 1 Chron. viii.38); and it is hardly coincidental that Sheba and his followers proceeded at once to Beth-maacah where, as we have seen, the family of Saul had connections.[16]

That Gibeon also continued to be an important religious centre during this reign is sufficiently established by the fact that, at the beginning of Solomon's reign, it was the greatest of the high places and the one to which the young king went for his inaugural dream- or vision-revelation (1 Kings iii.4). In view of the narrative which follows, it would be natural to suppose that it was at Gibeon that David 'sought the face of the Lord' (2 Sam. xxi.1) – a phrase which generally connotes a visit to a sanctuary – especially if this took place before the establishment of a provisional sanctuary in Jerusalem. Whether, as some scholars have proposed, Nathan received his temple-oracle at Gibeon (2 Sam. vii.4ff.) is more hypothetical but by no means impossible. The word of Yahweh came to him at night (verse 4) – according to Ps. lxxxix.19 in a vision – and it was in a dream by night that Solomon received the word of Yahweh. Noteworthy in this respect is the statement in *The*

*Lives of the Prophets* that Nathan was a Hivite from Gibeon and that it was in Gibeon that he was buried.[17] While we have no independent means of verifying this we have no grounds for denying it either; at least there is nothing in Old Testament tradition which explains how it could have arisen. The statements in the Chronicler which associate Zadok with Gibeon are much more problematic since the Chronicler has his own views on the cultic history of Israel prior to the building of the temple which are not necessarily based on evidence independent of older Israelite historical tradition.[18]

The narrative which is easily the most significant and informative with respect to Gibeon as a religious centre at this time is 2 Sam. xxi. 1–14, the ritual execution of the descendants of Saul. Structural analysis of 2 Sam. reveals quite clearly that xxi–xxiv form a series of appendices which break into the history of the succession to David's throne.[19] Despite the fact that this narrative has been written up, to some extent at least, as part of an *apologia* for David and his policies – his respect for Israel's treaty obligations and for the oath made to Jonathan are stressed – it is omitted from the Chronicler's history and was almost certainly absent from the Deuteronomist historical work.[20] We may reasonably suppose that the events narrated took place towards the beginning of the reign, about the time that David was taking steps to render Mephibaal, Saul's grandson, harmless.[21] The phrase *'aḥ<sup>a</sup>rē-ḵēn* at the end of the narrative (xxi. 14) is surprising since it generally serves as *incipit* to short narratives in series in 2 Sam.[22] Hence it may have introduced an episode following immediately after xxi. 1–14, either ix. 1ff. or some other which has not survived, and have been misplaced when the present narrative was arranged with others in the appendices.

We are therefore led to read xxi. 1–14 as one of a series of incidents describing how opposition from Saulites to David's rule was gradually eliminated. The following order may be suggested: 1 Sam. xxxi – 2 Sam. i, death of Saul and three of his sons; 2 Sam. iii. 26–39, assassination of Abner; iv. 5–12, assassination of Ishbaal; xxi. 1–14, execution of seven Saulites;

ix.1–13, measures taken to neutralize the influence of Mephibaal son of Jonathan. These might be understood as a chain of *Novellen*, a genre common in 1–2 Sam.,[23] though this designation should not prejudice the essential historicity of the narratives. With respect to the execution of the Saulites, we have the reference to the treaty and the oath, the consonance of this action with what we know of David's policy towards other ethnic groups, the naming of specific individuals,[24] the burial-place of Saul which seems to fit in well with indications of Saul's origins discussed earlier. We are therefore justified in concluding that we have here at least the nucleus of genuine historical tradition referring to events which took place towards the beginning of the reign. According to the order in 2 Sam., the capture of Jerusalem precedes the liberation of the region north-west of that city. The two accounts of the setting up of the first sanctuary in Jerusalem (vi.17; xxiv.18–25) and the renewed relevance of the Saulite claim with the defeat of the Philistines (v.17–25; viii.1*a*) would lead us to situate the parallel narratives in xxi.1–14 and xxiv at this time.[25] A protracted famine at the beginning of a reign the legitimacy of which was widely questioned could easily have been interpreted as a sign of the divine displeasure, and we know how solicitous David was to authenticate his rule by insisting on the return of Mikal and bringing the ark to Jerusalem. We may therefore see a close connection between the recent expulsion of the Philistines from the Gibeonite region (v.25), the establishment of a new religious centre in Jerusalem (vi–vii) and David's treatment of the remaining Saulites.

Historically, 2 Sam. xxi.1–14 is an important document bearing on the obscure reign of Saul, David's policy towards indigenous groups and the political and religious situation of the Gibeonites during this reign. With respect to the first, which we have already discussed, Saul's refusal to accept their incorporation by treaty into Israel (verse 5) and his hostility in general towards them (verses 2–3) are regarded as responsible for the curse to break which David requests a blessing (verse 3). It seems clear that David adopted a much more conciliatory and realistic policy towards 'Canaanite' elements than Saul. In Judges i.21, 27–33 we have a list of cities and territories which remained independent after the Settlement, including the Jebusites of the Hill Country, Beth-shemesh and other cities such as Aijalon in close proximity to Gibeon. These, together with other non-Israelite localities, were first incorporated into Israel, mostly by peaceful assimilation, under David.[26] Further evidence for his policy may be found in 2 Sam. xxiv.18ff., describing the setting up of the first cult-centre in Jerusalem on the threshing floor of the Jebusite Arauna.[27] This indicates a willingness to take over non-Israelite holy places and institutions, and other elements in pre-exilic Israelite worship may reflect non-Israelite cultic practices taken over by David.[28] It seems probable, moreover, that the new conception of kingship introduced by David owes a considerable debt to the Canaanite model.[29] In these and other respects his rule represents something quite new and his policy was quite the reverse of that of Saul which hardly went beyond the charismatic model of ruler illustrated in the book of Judges.

The same policy must have been applied to his relations with the Gibeonites, especially since we have explicit evidence in xxi.1–14 showing that he respected the terms under which they had entered into relations with Israel. By pursuing this policy he doubtless facilitated the eventual insertion of the Gibeonite cities into the eleventh administrative district of the twelve set up by Solomon (1 Kings iv.18) – at which poin they cease to have importance as a distinct enclave. If we are right in dating the Levitical cities to the time of David, their establishment may be seen as another measure undertaken by him aimed at the assimilation of 'Canaanite' regions. We recall that Gibeon is the first named of the four Levitical cities in Benjamin (Joshua xxi.17).[30]

Turning to the political status of the Gibeonites at the time of David, it is to be noted that the gloss in 2 Sam. xxi.2*b* states that they were not of the people of Israel – *lōʾ mibbᵉnê yiśrāʾēl.* This, together with their answer to David's query, shows that they regarded themselves as in some way integrated politically with Israel while remaining ethnically distinct and enjoying some degree of autonomy. As a result of the treaty they were incorporated *in some way* into Israel (*b*^e*qirbām*, Joshua x.1) and Saul had evidently sought to annul this incorporation by denying specific territorial rights guaranteed by treaty (*mēhiṯyaṣṣēḇ b*^e*ḵol g*^e*ḇûl yiśrā'ēl*, 2 Sam. xxi.5). That the incorporation was not complete emerges from the negotiations preceding the ritual execution. They first refused monetary compensation and the exaction of blood-vengeance, no doubt because they knew this latter alternative was not open to them.[31] Although the expiation is to be carried out cultically before the god of the tribal federation (verse 6), they clearly envisaged it as a different kind of expiation from that practised traditionally among the tribes; and in fact the only comparable act of which we have record is the execution of Israelite chiefs 'before the Lord' at Shittim (Num. xxv.4) which has some interesting similarities with the present narrative. We saw in an earlier chapter how the punishment inflicted on the Saulites has parallels in Hittite treaties from the fourteenth century.[32] Two conclusions, at any rate, are clear: that the Gibeonites as late as the time of David still evinced a strong sense of corporate identity which disappeared only in the following reign;[33] that their incorporation into Israel, while real and meaningful, did not give them equal rights with other Israelites but did imply more than the status of *gērîm* – mere 'hewers of wood and drawers of water' (Joshua ix.21, 23, 27; cf. Deut. xxix.10).

The absence of this episode from both the Deuteronomist historical work and the Chronicler's history, together with the apologetic gloss in xxi.2*b*, suggests disapproval of the Gibeonites' action from the religious point of view. At the same time, the efficacy of this cultic act is clearly acknowledged since 'God heeded supplications for the land' (verse 14) – no doubt by sending rain.[34]

That the execution is a cultic act is placed beyond reasonable doubt by the phrase 'before Yahweh', which also implies that it was carried out at a sanctuary. According to M.T. this was 'at Gibeah of Saul the chosen of Yahweh' (verse 6) and 'on the mountain' (verse 9). As we saw earlier, LXX has correctly preserved the reference to the Gibeonite sanctuary, and it would be reasonable to suggest that the narrative may ultimately derive from a Gibeonite tradition preserved at this sanctuary.[35] Here as elsewhere we have non-Israelite religious attitudes and practices thinly veneered with Yahwism. That the killing took place 'in the first days of harvest, at the beginning of the barley harvest' (verse 9) has suggested to some scholars that we have here in some way a re-enactment of the fertility myth widespread in Canaan.[36] The functional element in the myth is the need for rainfall to ripen the harvest, the failure of the late rains being disastrous for the agrarian economy of Syria and Palestine. In the Ugaritic Baal and Anath cycle Mot is killed by Anath between the harvest and the autumn rains, but the barley harvest is the crucial point in the seasonal drama.[37] It is argued that the form of execution, expressed by the rare verb *hwqʿ*, and the exposure of the corpses in the open until the rains came run parallel with the dismembering and exposing of the body of Mot in the Ugaritic texts.[38] The sackcloth worn by Rizpah is also reminiscent of sackcloth worn in mourning rites for the death of Baal, and in view of LXX ἐξηλιάσωμεν (for *hwqʿ*, verse 6) and the parallels with Num. xxv. 1–4 discussed earlier we should note the role of ŠMŠ in the fertility myth. It is he who 'burns for Mot', that is, ripens the corn and thus contributes to the death of Baal.[39] If the relevance of these parallels is accepted we would not necessarily have to conclude that the Gibeonites were of Canaanite stock. The seasonal myth was not the exclusive possession of Canaanites and we have evidence that the Hurrians, among others, took over the Semitic deities Dagan and ŠMŠ.[40]

It is beside the point to reject[41] this interpretation on the grounds that it runs counter to David's Yahwism. For one thing, David's Yahwism is not unambiguously attested, as we have seen, and in any case the association between the shedding of innocent blood and infertility was deeply imbedded in the ancient Near East and is reflected elsewhere in the Old Testament.[42] Moreover, it was the Gibeonites, not David, who carried out this rite, and they, as the narrator hastens to tell us, were not of the people of Israel. We conclude, therefore, that while it would be hazardous to press these resemblances too far, this reading of the narrative is consonant with the religious syncretism we should expect to be in currency among the Hivite Gibeonites (we may note, in passing, that more than fifty fertility figurines were discovered at el-Jîb).[43] This would go some way towards explaining the evident difficulties involved in their incorporation into Israel and the religious ambiguity surrounding the Gibeonite sanctuary.

It seems to us that the rivalry between the two cult-centres of Gibeon and Jerusalem, associated closely with Saul and David respectively, played a more important role in the religious history of Israel during the early monarchy than is generally recognized. 2 Sam. xxi.1–14 and xxiv contain parallel accounts of cultic acts carried out at Gibeon and Jerusalem respectively, the former at the barley harvest, the latter at the wheat harvest (xxi.9; xxiv.15). Both are successful and conclude in like manner: *wayyē'āṯēr 'ᵉlōhîm lā'āreṣ* (xxi.14), *wayyē'āṯēr YHWH lā'āreṣ* (xxiv.25). After the conclusion of the Succession History (1 Kings ii.46), which is interrupted by these chapters, there occurs at once the revelation to Solomon at Gibeon (1 Kings iii.4ff.) and, after the building of the temple, a parallel revelation at Jerusalem (ix.1–9: '...as he had appeared to him at Gibeon'). The two narratives reveal how undecided was the question of priority between the two. We might suppose, without being able to offer proof, that the second narrative had the purpose of legitimizing the new sanctuary to be established on the Jebusite threshing floor over against the renowned Gibeonite cult centre. Whether or not this is so, Gibeon continued to exert its fascination well into Solomon's reign. As we have seen, both David and Nathan probably continued to frequent Gibeon, though the ark and its tent-shrine were of obvious political and religious importance.[44] The inaugural sacrifice of David on the site where the temple was to be built did not prevent Solomon from sacrificing at Gibeon during the early part of his reign.

And it was there that his inaugural dream-revelation took place.

The theory has recently been defended that Solomon's reign was inaugurated not just by his revelation but also by his coronation at Gibeon.[45] M. Görg argues that the tent from which Zadok took the oil (1 Kings i.39) must be that in which Joab (ii.28) and probably also Adonijah (i.50) sought sanctuary, and that this tent and the altar it contained would hardly have been out in the open country (Gihon being the spring east of the city now known as 'Ain Sitti-Mariam). We must distinguish David's tent in Jerusalem from this other tent and we should hardly expect to find both in the same city. We should therefore think not of Gihon, which is nowhere else named in the Old Testament, but of Gibeon the sanctuary frequented by the first two Israelite kings.

Ingenious as it may be, this can hardly be considered a serious hypothesis. Even a rapid reading of 1 Kings i.32–53 shows that a site in or near Jerusalem is contemplated. Could Joab, who was certainly in Jerusalem, have heard the trumpet from Nebi Samwil about five miles distant (cf. verses 9, 42)? Quite apart from this, there is simply no time for a series of journeys back and forth between the two cities (cf. verses 50–3). That Gihon is nowhere else mentioned as a sacred place is not a good reason for eliminating it, and there is the striking fact, to which Görg does not allude, that Adonijah's coronation-feast also takes place at a water-source (i.9).

1 Kings iii.4–15*a* records that Solomon went to the Gibeonite sanctuary to offer sacrifice and narrates how he received in a dream a revelation deemed of key importance for the reign which was just beginning. The narrative is introduced in typically Deuteronomist fashion[46] and, as we should expect of the Deuteronomists, a note of reproof is detectable: 'Solomon loved Yahweh...*only* (*raq*) he sacrificed and burnt incense at the high places' (verse 3).[47] The reference is clearly to Gibeon described immediately afterwards as *the* great high place, but an excuse is offered in that the temple had not yet been built (verse 2). The parallel 2 Chron. i.3ff. justifies Solomon's

inaugural visit to Gibeon by the statement that the tent and the bronze altar were located there.

Evidence for Deuteronomistic editorial activity in 1 Kings iii.4–15 does not by any means exclude the possibility that an ancient tradition has been preserved here. What is remarkable, on the contrary, is that the Deuteronomists did not suppress Solomon's associations with this great pre-Israelite sanctuary.[48] The concluding statement about Solomon's return to Jerusalem and worship before the ark (verse 15) probably has the purpose of stressing his 'orthodoxy' *despite* the visit to Gibeon.[49] The placing of this incident immediately after the conclusion of the Succession History is not accidental. The kingdom was now at last established in the hand of Solomon (ii.46*b*) but his rule was legitimized neither by a covenant, as was David's, nor by personal charisma or proven aptitude for governing. The purpose of the present narrative was to provide this legitimation, as is clear from Solomon's opening words (verses 6–8). This at once brings out the parallelism between this account and the narrative-complex 2 Sam. vi–viii – the establishment of the ark in Jerusalem and the oracle of Nathan – which provided the theological rationale for David's rule. What is significant for our theme here is that in both cases Gibeon plays an important role: the ark-god, who had chosen to reside in a Gibeonite city, transferred his abode to Jerusalem, and it may have been at Gibeon that Nathan received his oracle; Solomon's rule is given divine authentication not at Jerusalem, as we might have expected, but at Gibeon. In our view this would greatly strengthen the hypothesis that the 'great high place' had been a royal sanctuary before Solomon and Gibeon a royal city.[50]

The parallels between this inaugural visit to a sanctuary, with the request for an oracle and the bestowal of virtues and aptitudes necessary for ruling, and Egyptian royal protocol have often been noted.[51] A particularly close example may be found in the so-called Sphinx stele of Thutmoses IV to whom a god comes in a dream just before his accession and promises him the kingdom and great riches.[52] This is only one of many cultural contacts between Egypt and Israel at this time, and we may note in passing the evidence for the same from the excavations at el-Jîb.[53] There can be no doubt that, despite the presence of the ark in Jerusalem, Gibeon was considered the most suitable place for this sacral act suggested by well known Egyptian practice.

According to 1 Kings iii.5, the giver of the revelation is Yahweh, though it is *'elōhîm* who then goes on to speak. In Canaanite religious texts El comes to his devotees, including the king, in dreams, it is through the king that he communicates his revelations and he is represented as the dispenser of wisdom.[54] Though here we are told only that the god appeared to Solomon in a dream by night, it is possible that Solomon was practising the ritual *incubatio* attested in Canaan and the ancient Near East in general.[55] Whether or not this is the case, evidence is not lacking for religious syncretism in Israelite life at this time. The ritual act described in 2 Sam. xxi.1–14 takes place 'before Yahweh' yet clearly it is not a Yahwist practice but rather of a kind attested in the religious milieu of Canaan. Hence it is reasonable to suppose that, in the first instance, the deity who revealed himself was identified as an El-hypostasis and that the assimilation to Yahweh is due to the religious scruple of the redactor.[56]

After the building of the Jerusalem temple 'Yahweh appeared to Solomon a second time, as he had appeared to him at Gibeon' (1 Kings ix.2). This revelation gave the final blessing of authenticity to the new cult centre and implied the definitive eclipse of Gibeon by its more powerful rival. Its fame lingered on into the exilic period and beyond, as we shall see, but it no longer had a major role to play. With the administrative reforms of Solomon, his use of non-Israelite elements for his many building projects and perhaps also the transfer of cultic personnel from Gibeon to Jerusalem, the existence of the Gibeonite cities as a distinct political and ethnic unit came to an end.

CHAPTER VIII

# THE GIBEONITE SANCTUARY IN LATER SOURCES

For any mention of Gibeon in the Old Testament after the death of Solomon we have to come down to the exilic period when Johanan encountered Ishmael, assassin of the Babylonian governor Gedaliah, 'at the great pool which is in Gibeon' (Jer. xli. 12 cf. verse 16). During this long period of time the only reference to the city in any other text known to us is the list of Palestinian cities captured during Sheshonk's campaign (ca. 924 B.C.).[1] Jeremiah mentions two Yahwist prophets from Gibeonite cities: Uriah ben-Shemaiah of Kiriath-jearim (xxvi. 20–3) and Hananiah ben-Azzur of Gibeon (xxviii. 1ff.). The name of this last, together with several other seventh-century Israelite names, has been found among the el-Jîb inscriptions.[2] All four Gibeonite cities are listed among those resettled after the Exile (Neh. vii. 25, 29 = Ezra ii. 20, 25) and the men of Gibeon, including a certain Meletiah, worked on the reconstruction of the Jerusalem wall together with men from Mizpah (Neh. iii. 7).[3]

Mention of Mizpah raises again the question discussed briefly in the opening chapter. It was suggested that some of the Old Testament references to Benjaminite Mizpah may in fact be identical with the Gibeonite sanctuary.[4] In one strand of Judges xx–xxi (the crime of the men of Gibeah and its punishment) the central sanctuary is Mizpah where the Israelite confederates come together in their war against Benjamin.[5] There is good reason to believe that this strand comes from the same milieu and time as the Mizpah narratives in 1 Sam. which represent a late stage of redaction and are in general historically untrustworthy.[6] The problem of identifying Benjaminite Mizpah, discussed inconclusively for decades, has been further obscured by the fact that many scholars have felt obliged to support exclusively the claim of either Tell en-

Naṣbeh or Nebi Samwil, the only serious contenders. Those who opt for the former rightly make much of 1 Kings xv.22 (=2 Chron. xvi.6) which describes how Asa fortified Geba of Benjamin and Mizpah against Baasha. Admitting for the moment that this does refer to Tell en-Naṣbeh,[7] it does not thereby follow that this identification can be posited for every Old Testament occurrence of Mizpah. The references in Judges and 1 Sam. would, in particular, apply much more readily to Nebi Samwil, especially in view of the name which presupposes an association with Samuel and the negative conclusions from the excavation of Tell en-Naṣbeh.[8] The Mizpah of the exilic period referred to in 2 Kings xxv.23ff. and Jer. xl–xli was certainly thought to be identical with the city fortified by Asa – this is clear from the reference to the cistern in Jer. xli.9 – and practically all modern scholars identify it with Tell en-Naṣbeh.[9] Here again, however, the texts in question prove refractory in some important respects. For one thing, the prophet Jeremiah is told to *return* from Ramah to Mizpah (Jer. xl.5) and this verb would hardly be appropriate for a journey northward.[10] More important, we read in Jer. xli.10ff. that Ishmael, who had set out from Mizpah in the direction of Amman, was met by Johanan and his army at Gibeon, that is, south-south-west of Tell en-Naṣbeh; and it is difficult to believe that he would have gone in practically the opposite direction to Amman when he was so desperately in need of time to escape after the assassination.[11] This difficulty is eliminated if the starting-point is thought of as Nebi Samwil.

One of the principal arguments in favour of Tell en-Naṣbeh is that the men on their way to the temple-site in Jerusalem who had set out from Shechem, Shiloh and Samaria (Jer. xli.5) would naturally travel along the main north–south road on which Tell en-Naṣbeh is situated. If however, as is surely possible, they had to obtain permission from Gedaliah at Mizpah before proceeding to Jerusalem, this argument loses its force. We may add that the name *hammiṣpāh* (watch-tower) is not particularly well suited to Tell en-Naṣbeh which has not a striking elevation and is surrounded by hills some of which are higher than it. Such a name would be much more suited to Nebi Samwil which provides an unobstructed view in all directions. Moreover, Neh. iii.7 and possibly also Jer. xli.11ff. suggest a close connection between Mizpah and Gibeon which is more easily explained by the Nebi Samwil hypothesis. Whatever arguments are drawn from the results of Badè's excavations at Tell en-Naṣbeh in favour of this site as against Nebi Samwil are offset by the discovery that the city gate faced north not south – which would be very strange indeed if this were the Mizpah fortified against the Northern Kingdom by Asa.[12] In short, the identification of Mizpah in the exilic period with Tell en-Naṣbeh is not nearly so assured as is often claimed.

In the second century B.C. a Mizpah was known which had been a 'place of prayer' and which was situated opposite (κατέναντι) Jerusalem (1 Macc. iii.46). A survey of the use of this preposition in the Greek versions shows that it implies proximity and, generally, visibility. This is eminently true of Nebi Samwil with respect to Jerusalem and not at all of Tell en-Naṣbeh.[13] This text would therefore provide valuable confirmation of a continuous tradition about the Gibeonite high place, though it eventually came to be associated with Samuel rather than Saul – for reasons which are not difficult to understand.

It must be emphasized before leaving this question that the evidence is not decisively in favour of either site and that the problem of Benjaminite Mizpah must remain under study. We would suggest tentatively that both sites acquired this name at different times,[14] that Nebi Samwil was known in the earlier period as *haggiḇ'āh*, later as *hammiṣpāh*,[15] and that the memory of its cultic prestige was never wholly submerged.

We must now turn to the Chronicler who gives an important place to Gibeon in his reconstruction of the cultic history of early Israel (1 Chron. xvi.39; xxi.29; 2 Chron. i.3, 13). Before considering his use of sources and his own contribution we should first look at some aspects of the Priestly corpus since the Chronicler is clearly familiar with the Priestly understanding of cult and the cultic history of Israel. We are referring particularly to the Priestly treatment of the ark and the tent.[16]

According to P the construction of the ark is entrusted by Moses to Bezalel (Exod. xxv. 10ff.; xxxvii. 1ff.). Its proper place is in the tent, it appears first in certain narratives dealing with the desert period and the Conquest and is then located in the Jerusalem temple. The tent, however, is clearly considered to be more important than the ark. Built under the direction of Moses according to divine prescription (Exod. xxiv. 8f.; xxvi. 1ff.; xxxvi. 8ff.), it stood in the centre of the camp during the desert period as the locus of Yahweh's self-revelation. After the Conquest it was situated at Shiloh (Joshua xviii. 1; xix. 51)[17] and later in the temple, and it is clear that the description of the tent as an early Israelite sanctuary is based on the temple.[18] The tent which houses the ark is thought of as a permanent sanctuary: the temple itself is often referred to as *'ōhel* which means 'dwelling place' rather than specifically a tent.[19] This observation, elementary as it is, may explain why later tradition located the tent at Shiloh despite the clear indications in early sources that the Shiloh sanctuary was a permanent temple.[20] It seems a reasonable hypothesis that the Priestly concept of the tent is a combination of this retrojection from the temple with the Tent of Meeting mentioned in early Pentateuchal sources.[21]

Turning to the Chronicler, we find much in common with the Priestly writer and also some significant divergencies and additions. For our purpose, the most important of these is the notice that the Mosaic tent was located at Gibeon before the building of the Jerusalem temple (1 Chron. xvi. 39; xxi. 29; 2 Chron. i. 3ff.). The entire work of the Chronicler is centred on temple worship, perhaps with a view to the religious and political determination of the Jewish community over against the Samaritans.[22] This climactic event in Israel's history (the building of the temple) was prepared for by David, who is presented as the organizer of the Jerusalem cult and its personnel, particularly the Levites and singers.[23] The information which the Chronicler provides on the early cultic history of Israel is incomplete and sometimes vague and contradictory. Following 1–2 Sam., he gives greater importance to the ark than the Priestly writer does. It lay neglected at Kiriath-jearim during the reign of Saul (1 Chron. xiii. 3; cf. 1 Sam. vii. 1f.), was brought by David from that city to the house of Obed-edom the Gittite (xiii. 13f.) and was thence, after an interval during which the Philistines were defeated near Gibeon, brought to Jerusalem where it was placed in a tent (xv. 25ff.). In due course Solomon installed it in the newly built temple (2 Chron. v. 2).

It will be noted that here the Chronicler follows 1–2 Sam. quite closely. The only significant divergencies are the location of the Uzzah episode (the threshing floor of Chidon, xiii. 9), the explanation of the delay in bringing it to Jerusalem,[24] and the ordering of events between the first and second stages of its progress from Kiriath-jearim to its final resting place. The most surprising addition to what we know from early sources is that for the Chronicler the 'tabernacle of Yahweh' together with the altar of burnt offering made by Bezalel were at Gibeon at the time of the transference of the ark to Jerusalem. Most scholars have seen this as a pure fabrication designed to justify Solomon's inaugural visit to Gibeon and bring his conduct in line with the Priestly law in Lev. xvii. 8–9.[25] Such an interpretation seems to be confirmed by the difficulty the Chronicler experienced in allocating cult personnel to the two shrines: in 1 Chron. vi. 31f. the Levites are all without distinction in the service of the ark and the tent, while in xvi. 37ff. Asaphites and others minister to the ark and Zadokites are in charge of the tent at Gibeon. But before we can evaluate this specific contribution of the Chronicler we have to look at the total view of the early cult of Israel which is expressed in his work.

In the first place, the Chronicler follows P in tracing the essential elements of Israelite worship back to Moses. In particular, he presupposes the Mosaic origins of ark and tent which were ideally, if not always historically, inseparable. One of his major concerns is to delineate David as the founder of the Jerusalem cultus and to establish essential continuity between this new and decisive stage of development and the earlier history. The religious ideal had always been one sanctuary, comprising ark and tent, but something had gone wrong in the period between Shiloh and Jerusalem, especially during the reign of Saul when the ark had been neglected (1 Chron. xiii.3). This was finally rectified when both ark and tent were solemnly installed in the Jerusalem temple by Solomon (2 Chron. v.5). The difficulty which he evidently experiences with the interim period seems to arise from his reliance on the tradition of the ark's stay at Kiriath-jearim (1 Chron. xiii.5; cf. 1 Sam. vii.2) together with the other tradition, still alive, of Gibeon as a great cult-centre at the time of the early monarchy. For him the greatness of David is seen above all in his restoration of correct worship after a period of infidelity for which Saul was chiefly responsible (1 Chron. x.13f.).

For the Chronicler the Mosaic tent, for which he uses several designations,[26] was at Gibeon for a period down to the early reign of Solomon. The *terminus a quo* of this period is not stated but it ended once the temple of Jerusalem was completed (2 Chron. v.5).[27] The temple musicians founded by David functioned *lipnê miškan 'ōhel mô'ēḏ* at Gibeon before being transferred to the house of Yahweh in Jerusalem at the time of Solomon (1 Chron. vi.16f. [M.T.]).[28] Levites and Zadokites also operated at this same *miškan bêṯ 'ᵉlōhîm*, the latter being responsible for the sacrificial cultus at the altar of burnt offering, the bronze altar made by Bezalel, which was also there (1 Chron. vi.33f. [M.T.]).[29] That the Chronicler endows the Zadokite priesthood with an Aaronite genealogy (cf. vi.38 [M.T.]) is very significant even though difficult to accept as a historical statement.[30] It may, perhaps, be not wholly unconnected with the names of cultic personnel associated with the ark during its stay in a Gibeonite city and the fact that Gibeon is one of the Levitical cities set aside for the sons of Aaron (Joshua xxi.13–19).[31]

We might anticipate some confusion arising between the Mosaic tent at Gibeon and the tent which David set up for the ark as a temporary measure in Zion; in fact, a glossator goes to pains to point out the difference between the two in the account of Solomon's visit to Gibeon (2 Chron. i.4). The Chronicler felt the difficulty that David should have brought the ark to Jerusalem while leaving the tent at Gibeon. His explanation is that David was prevented from going to Gibeon by the angel of Yahweh (1 Chron. xxi.29f.) – though nothing prevented Solomon from going there (2 Chron. i.3ff.) – and this may imply that the tent set up in Jerusalem was a temporary substitute for the Mosaic tent at Gibeon. Both here and elsewhere it is not too difficult to see how the Chronicler's presuppositions and points of view have led him to rewrite the history, yet it would be unjustified to go on from this to deny *any* historical value to his work at this point. It seems to us reasonably assured that Gibeon was a great cult-centre down to the reign of Solomon and that David did play an important part in laying the foundations of the Jerusalem cult. More in particular, it seems reasonable to accept that the new cultic situation came about in two stages: the transference of the ark from a Gibeonite to a Jebusite city (1 Chron. xiii–xvi), the building of the temple which resulted in the definitive supersession of the Gibeonite sanctuary (2 Chron. v.5). The record has been obscured by polemical factors touched on more than once in this study and by the particular theological viewpoints of the Chronicler himself (especially his understanding of ark and tent inherited from the Priestly corpus); yet, despite this, the main outline of events can still be discerned.[32]

Later Jewish tradition, attested principally in the Babylonian Talmud, has combined the data provided by the Priestly writer and the Chronicler to form a more or less consistent account of cultic history before the building of the temple. Here too the tent rather than the ark is in the foreground, and for the same reasons. One tractate summarizes the history as follows: 'It was taught: when Eli the priest died, Shiloh was destroyed and they repaired to Nob...Nob was destroyed and they went to Gibeon.'[33] According to this Talmudic tradition the tent remained at Shiloh three hundred and seventy years and at Nob and Gibeon combined fifty-seven years; while, following 1 Sam. vii.2, the ark was at Kiriath-jearim twenty years but never at Nob or Gibeon.[34] What is of interest here is not the chronological indication, which has no independent value for history, but the fact of three 'divine residences' before the building of the temple (called 'the permanent house') and the close historical connection presupposed between Shiloh and Nob on the one hand and Nob and Gibeon on the other.[35] The Talmudic tradition also follows the Priestly writer and Chronicler in making these three tent-sanctuaries places of sacrifice with an altar: 'Rabbi Hisda said: the altar at Shiloh was of stones. For it was taught, Rabbi Eleazar ben-Jacob said, why is *stones* stated three times? One refers to that of Shiloh, another to that of Nob and Gibeon, and the third to that of the Eternal House.'[36] This follows the Priestly view of Shiloh as tent-temple, the Chronicler's understanding of Gibeon as tent-sanctuary and also, probably, the mention of 'the great stone which is at Gibeon' (2 Sam. xx.8) understood as an altar. Inclusion of Nob here and elsewhere is probably due to assimilation of this sanctuary with David's tent (1 Sam. xvii.54; xxi.9; 2 Sam. vi.17) which was then identified with the tent-sanctuary at Gibeon. In some passages in the Talmud Nob and Gibeon seem to be identified but for the most part they are distinguished as successive stages in the early cultic history of Israel.

These scattered attestations in Talmudic tradition are, as far as can be seen, almost entirely dependent on interpretation of biblical texts and therefore cannot be used as primary source-material. But even though they contain unverifiable assertions about the Gibeonite sanctuary – that it was Yahwist from the beginning, that it contained the Mosaic tent, that it was a synagogue[37] – they do confirm the crucial importance of Gibeon between the destruction of Shiloh and the establishment of the Jerusalem sanctuary. Whether Gibeon was an important sanctuary before this time, as the Chronicler seems to suppose, can hardly be established or even discussed in the absence of evidence.[38]

A further link between the Gibeonites and post-exilic cult and cultic ideas is that group of temple-servants called *nethinim*. The genealogical lists in 1 Chron. i–ix end with four categories into which the entire community is divided: Israel (i.e. the laity), the priests, Levites, *nethinim*.[39] This is practically identical with Neh. xi.3–21 and appears to be based on this latter which, however, adds 'the sons of Solomon's servants', a class closely connected with the *nethinim* as is clear from Neh. vii.46–59 = Ezra ii.43–57. It would be reasonable to suppose that 1 Chron. ix.2 is a later version of Neh. xi.3 made at a time when 'the sons of Solomon's servants' had ceased to exist independently of the *nethinim*.[40] The fact that the Chronicler repeats the Gibeonite 'genealogy' (viii.29–40) immediately after the *nethinim* (ix.35–44) will at once suggest some association between the latter and Gibeonites; such an association is in fact taken for granted in later Jewish tradition.

This lowest class of temple personnel occurs only in post-exilic sources.[41] They are among those who returned from exile (Ezra ii.43 = Neh. vii.46) and settled in their own cities as opposed to priests and Levites who lived in Jerusalem. In the parallel Neh. vii.73, however, *all* classes lived in their own cities, while according to Neh. iii.26 and xi.21 there were *nethinim* living on Ophel who had a house opposite the Miphkad Gate (iii.31). If they were constituted as a class only after the Exile, as the absence of the term in pre-exilic sources might indicate,[42] we still have to explain how the association between Gibeonites and *nethinim* arose. According to Ezra viii.20 they were instituted by David, founder of the temple cult, to attend on the Levites. Another tradition (Num. xxxi.30, 47) has it that Moses and Eleazar the priest 'gave' them (*nāṭan*) to the Levites in their service of the tent. In Joshua ix, the account of the Gibeonite treaty, the last redactional stratum deals with the fate of the Gibeonites as 'hewers of wood and drawers of water'; they were given over by Joshua for the service of 'the house of my God' (verse 23) and 'the altar of Yahweh' (verse 27), and so they remained up to the time of writing (verse 27). 'This day' may well refer to the exilic or immediate post-exilic period in view of the way the *nethinim* are presented in Chron. and Ezra–Nehemiah.[43]

In the classification of the whole people as a cultic community in post-exilic sources, especially 1 Chron. ix, it is clear that the *nethinim* are distinct from gatekeepers, other temple guards and singers.[44] The remark in 1 Chron. ix. 33 that the Levitical singers were free from other service makes this abundantly clear and obliges us to conclude that, for the Chronicler, the Gibeonites whose genealogy follows were identical with the *nethinim* or temple servants. It would be interesting in this respect to compare this classification of groups within the community with that in Deut. reflecting an earlier historical stage, probably the seventh or sixth century. Here, too, the community is 'Israel', there are priests and Levites with well defined functions, and though no reference is made to *nethinim*, Deut. xxix. 10 defines 'hewers of wood and drawers of water' as *gēr bᵉqereḇ maḥᵃnēka.*[45] There is clearly some affinity between the *gērîm* as understood by Deut. and the post-exilic *nethinim.*

On an overall view of the evidence, there seems no reason at all to doubt an historical nexus between Gibeonites and *nethinim*. As we have seen, the Gibeonites retained their identity and a certain degree of autonomy into the reign of David and some of them certainly officiated at the Gibeonite sanctuary. This situation came to an end with the administrative reforms of Solomon and his use of non-Israelite groups – including Amorites and Hivites – in forced-labour gangs.[46] Once the Gibeonite sanctuary had been definitely eclipsed by its rival in Jerusalem, it is entirely probable that Gibeonites and other ethnic groups were used for the many menial tasks involved in the sacrificial cultus, and the phrase 'hewers of wood and drawers of water' would be consistent with such occupations. At the time of Ezekiel there were foreigners, *bᵉnê-nēḵār*, serving in the temple;[47] a piece of information which provides a valuable link with the *nethinim* of the post-exilic period. In the immediate post-exilic period the *nethinim* were clearly distinguished from those engaged in forced labour, including work on the temple.[48] Although most of the names of *nethinim* recorded in Ezra–Nehemiah are non-Jewish (as are those in 1 Chron. ix.35–44), we find all the people, including the *nethinim*, engaging in a covenant to keep the law with regard to separation from 'the peoples of the land' (Neh. x.28ff.). This too was clearly in the spirit of Deuteronomy.

In the Talmud 'Gibeonite' is generally equated with *nathin*.[49] Various reasons are given for their inferior status vis-à-vis Israelites: they were vengeful in exacting tribute of blood, their circumcision was invalid, they had been forbidden marriage with Israelites either by Moses or David.[50] All these are deductions from biblical texts rather than non-biblical tradition, though the reference to their circumcision may be interesting in view of the possible relevance of Joshua v.2–9 to the Gibeonite question.[51] In one text they are put in the same category as the 'bastards' of the Deuteronomic community rule (Deut. xxiii.2), implying that full membership of the cultic community was denied them.[52] In general, however, there is nothing significant in this late tradition, carried down into the Gemara period, which takes us behind the historical reconstruction of post-exilic orthodoxy.

## NOTES TO CHAPTER I (pp. 1–13)

1. J. B. Pritchard, *Hebrew Inscriptions and Stamps from Gibeon*, Philadelphia, 1959, pp. 1–27.
2. M.T. has *bᵉgiḇʿaṯ šāʾûl*, cf. verse 9: *bᵉhar lipnē YHWH*. With practically all commentators we read *gibʿôn* in verse 6 following LXX^BA, Aquila and Symm.
3. Many commentators have found *derek miḏbar giḇʿôn* (verse 24) difficult to accept and substitute *geḇaʿ* for *giḇʿôn*. This, however, may depend on a rather narrow interpretation of *miḏbar*. See M. du Buit, *Géographie de la Terre Sainte*, Paris, 1958, pp. 102f.; J. Simons, *The Geographical and Topographical Texts of the Old Testament*, Leiden, 1959, pars. 744–6.
4. Emending 2 Sam. v.25 M.T. from *miggeḇaʿ* to *miggiḇʿôn* following LXX^BA, 1 Chron. xiv.16 and Isa. xxviii.21 which mentions Perazim (cf. 2 Sam. v.20) and the valley of Gibeon.
5. 2 Sam. v.25 and xxi.6.
6. Particularly in Judges xix–xx, 1 Sam. x.5, 10, xiii.3 and the crucial texts which speak of the ark being left *baggiḇʿāh* (R.S.V. 'on the hill') in 1 Sam. vii.1 and 2 Sam. vi.3, 4.
7. *A.N.E.T.*, pp. 263–4, 242–3.
8. J. B. Pritchard, op. cit., pp. 1–27; *S.V.T.*, vii (1960), p. 1; *B.A.S.O.R.*, clx (1960), pp. 2ff.; on a more popular level *Gibeon Where the Sun Stood Still*, Princeton, 1962, p. 46.
9. *Z.D.P.V.*, lxxiii (1957), p. 10.
10. A. T. Olmstead, *History of Syria and Palestine*, New York, 1931, pp. 354–6; Y. Aharoni, *The Land of the Bible*, London, 1966, pp. 283–8; M. Mazar, *S.V.T.*, iv (1957), pp. 57–66, who suggests a *boustrophedon* reading; A. Alt, *K.S.*, II, 79f.
11. *Ant.* 7 11 7; *War* 2 19 1. The stadium is about 185 metres.
12. Illustrated by the campaigns of the Crusaders (F. M. Abel, *J.P.O.S.*, xi (1931), pp. 141–3), the British campaigns against the Turks during the First World War and the recent Israeli–Arab war on the second day of which (6 June 1967) it was occupied by Israeli forces.
13. *Onomasticon* 66, 11ff.; A. Alt, *P.J.B.*, xxii (1926), pp. 1ff.; *Z.D.P.V.*, lxix (1953), pp. 1–27. See also on this question G. Beyer, *Z.D.P.V.*, liii (1930), pp. 199ff.; F. M. Abel, *R.B.*, xliii (1934), pp. 349ff.; M. Noth, *Z.D.P.V.*, lxvi (1943), pp. 32ff.; C. U. Wolf, *B.A.*, xxvii (1964), pp. 66ff.
14. Art. cit. (note 13), pp. 352f.
15. Jerome, *Epitaphium Sanctae Paulae*, cap. VIII; Eusebius, *Adv. Haer.*, XLVI, 5.
16. Peter was evidently thinking of Gadera, as also Antonius Placentinus in his *Itinerarium*, 163. See P. Geyer (ed.), *Itinera Hierosolymitana saec. IIII–VIII* in *Corpus Script. Eccl. Lat.*, Vienna, 1898, p. 39.
17. K. Elliger, *Z.D.P.V.*, lxxiii (1957), pp. 125ff.; id., *Mélanges bibliques rédigés en l'honneur de André Robert*, Paris, 1957, pp. 82ff.; R. T. O'Callaghan, *Bib.*, xxxii (1951), pp. 57ff.
18. *Biblical Researches in Palestine*, II, Boston, 1874, 456. On Robinson's work see F. M. Abel, *J.B.L.*, lviii (1939), pp. 366f.
19. See G. Kampffmeyer, *Z.D.P.V.*, xvi (1893), pp. 26f.; K. Elliger, art. cit., p. 128.
20. Before the excavations it was accepted by G. Dalman, *P.J.B.*, xxi (1925), pp. 58ff.; xxii (1926), pp. 104ff.; *Jerusalem und sein Gelände*, Gütersloh, 1930, pp. 218ff.; Abel, art. cit., pp. 341ff.; *Géographie de la Palestine*, II, Paris, 1938, 419; R. de Vaux, *Les Livres de Samuel* (2nd edn), Paris, 1961, p. 153. Also Noth, *S.V.T.*, vii (1960), p. 273; Albright, *B.A.S.O.R.*, clix (1960), p. 37. Elliger, art. cit., p. 132, and Simons, op. cit., pp. 175f. remain unconvinced.

21. *Hebrew Inscriptions and Stamps from Gibeon*, p. 9.
22. *Gibeon Where the Sun Stood Still*, p. 79; W. L. Reed, in D. Winton Thomas (ed.), *Archaeology and Old Testament Study*, Oxford, 1967, pp. 237f. K. Galling, *B.O.*, xxii (1965), pp. 244–5, has challenged this interpretation.
23. Pritchard, *S.V.T.*, vii (1960), pp. 8ff. H. J. Franken and C. A. Franken-Battershill, *A Primer of Old Testament Archaeology*, Leiden, 1963, pp. 110–14, have questioned Pritchard's chronology and suggest further work needs to be done, especially on the stepped tunnel, towards determining the date of construction.
24. *B.A.S.O.R.*, clxxviii (1965), p. 71.
25. *Gibeon where the Sun stood still*, pp. 159f.
26. The same conclusion is drawn by Elliger, art. cit., pp. 131f., and K. D. Schunck, *Benjamin*, Berlin, 1963, p. 133, n. 123.
27. Pritchard, art. cit., p. 6; H. Vincent, *R.B.*, xxxi (1922), p. 366. R. Brinker, *The Influence of Sanctuaries in Early Israel*, Manchester, 1946, p. 157, emends to *habbāmāh hagg*[e]*dôlāh*, but this is pure speculation.
28. The presence of a mosque has made it impossible to excavate Nebi Samwil and settle the question one way or the other. Professor Pritchard informed me by letter that in February 1968 he visited the site and looked unsuccessfully for Iron Age pottery. Pottery remains may, however, have been washed away or lie under the mosque and adjoining building on the east side. Early attempts to excavate part of the site were carried out too unscientifically to be of any use. On these see P. Löhmann, *Z.D.P.V.*, xli (1918), pp. 117ff.; L. H. Vincent, *R.B.*, xxxi (1922), pp. 362ff. Nebi Samwil as the Gibeonite sanctuary is accepted by H. Vincent; F. M. Savignac and F. M. Abel, *R.B.*, xxi (1912), pp. 267ff.; H. W. Hertzberg, *Z.A.W.*, vi (1929), p. 191; G. Dalman, op. cit., pp. 62f.; M. J. Lagrange, *R.B.*, i (1892), p. 455; de Vaux, op. cit., p. 233, and tentatively by Pritchard himself. It is questioned by J. Simons, op. cit., p. 327, and J. A. Soggin, *Z.A.W.*, lxxviii (1966), p. 190, n. 25.
29. J. Simons, op. cit., p. 176; Aharoni, op. cit., p. 375.
30. J. A. Knudtzon, *Die El-Amarna-Tafeln*, Leipzig, 1915, No. 273; S. A. B. Mercer, *The Tell El-Amarna Tablets*, II, Toronto, 1939, 686ff.
31. H. Bauer, *Z.D.M.G.*, lxxiv (1920), pp. 210f.; Alt, *K.S.*, I, 107, n. 6. In view of the hypothesis, advanced later on, that the Gibeonites had some affinity with the Hurrians, it may be of interest to note that Pirigal, the lioness-goddess, is mentioned in the Hurrian foundation tablet of Tišari. Text in A. Parrot and J. Nougayrol, *R.A.*, xlii (1948), pp. 1–20.
32. The identification with el-Jîb was defended by L. Heidet, *R.B.*, iii (1894), pp. 321ff.; Alt, *P.J.B.*, xxii (1926), pp. 11ff.; id., *Z.D.P.V.*, lxix (1953), pp. 1ff.; Noth, *Z.D.P.V.*, lxvi (1943), pp. 32ff.; id., *Z.D.P.V.*, lxxiii (1957), pp. 7ff.; Galling, *Biblisches Reallexikon*, Tübingen, 1937, p. 195; Elliger, art. cit., pp. 125ff. Albright proposed Tell en-Naṣbeh, *J.B.L.*, lviii (1939), p. 180; lix (1940), p. 541.
33. *Eretz-Israel*, iii (1954), pp. 111ff.
34. Robinson, op. cit., I, 452; Abel, op. cit., II, 262; de Vaux, op. cit., p. 161; M. Haran, *V.T.*, xi (1961), p. 160; du Buit, op. cit., pp. 163f.
35. See J. M. Myers, *I Chronicles*, Garden City, N.Y., 1965, p. 55.
36. As proposed by Alt, *P.J.B.*, xxxv (1939), pp. 100–4; B. Mazar, *I.E.J.*, iv (1954), pp. 227ff.
37. As we shall see, there is some overlap between Gibeonite and Edomite names. A place-name *gam-ti-e-ti* occurs in an Amarna letter from the lord of Gezer (Knudtzon, op. cit., No. 295) and a similar *gi-im-ti* in the account of Sargon's campaign against the Philistines (*A.N.E.T.*, p. 286; cf. p. 489). The Githam of the *Onomasticon* appears to be distinct from the Gitta of the Madaba map.

38. In Joshua ix.17, LXX[B] has πόλεις Ιαρειν, LXX[A] πόλεις Ιαρειμ, and Vulg. *Cariathiarim* (cf. LXX[B] Καριαθιαρειν, and LXX[A] Καριαθιαριμ in xviii.14). There are minor differences in spelling in different places in the LXX.
39. Kallai-Kleinmann, *V.T.*, viii (1958), pp. 134ff., interprets the *giḇʿaṯ qiryaṯ* of Joshua xviii.28 as referring to a new Judahite quarter built on to the old city after Benjamin had been absorbed into Judah; it is this which is referred to in xviii.14 as 'the city of the sons of Judah'. See also Aharoni, *V.T.*, ix (1959), pp. 225ff. But this reading leaves us with only thirteen instead of fourteen cities as demanded by the final summary, xviii.28, and we might add that *gibʿaṯ qiryaṯ* does not look very likely as a city-name.
40. See Noth, *Das Buch Josua* (2nd edn), Tübingen, 1953, pp. 89f.
41. Both Hebron (Joshua xiv.13; Judges i.20) and Debir (Joshua xv.15–19; Judges i.11–15) were settled by Calebite clans. The Chronicler's genealogies would presuppose that the population of Kiriath-jearim at some stage had Calebite affinities also (1 Chron. ii.50*b*).
42. See Alt, *P.J.B.*, xxi (1925), pp. 100ff., and *K.S.*, II, 276ff.; F. M. Cross and G. E. Wright, *J.B.L.*, lxv (1956), pp. 202ff., M. Noth, op. cit., pp. 99, 109ff., and *Z.D.P.V.*, lviii (1935), pp. 185ff.; Albright, *Z.A.W.*, xliv (1926), pp. 236f.; *J.B.L.*, lvii (1938), p. 226; Kallai-Kleinmann, *V.T.*, viii (1958), pp. 134ff.; id., xi (1961), pp. 223–7; *I.E.J.*, vi (1956), p. 187; Aharoni, *V.T.*, ix (1959), pp. 225ff.
43. Op. cit., pp. 286f.; art. cit., p. 229. Cf. the reference to Kiriath-jearim as the site of a Danite encampment in Judges xviii.12.
44. At the time of Solomon the Jerusalem province was under the Benjaminite Shimei ben-Ela, 1 Kings iv.18. See Albright, *J.P.O.S.*, v (1925), pp. 16f.; *Archaeology and the Religion of Israel* (3rd edn), Baltimore, 1953, p. 141.
45. Mazar, *S.V.T.*, iv (1957), p. 61; Aharoni, op. cit., p. 287.
46. Robinson, op. cit., I, 446; Dalman, op. cit., pp. 214, 224; Abel, op. cit., II, 56; Simons, op. cit., p. 151; H. Vincent, *R.B.*, iv (1907), pp. 414ff.; S. Lauffs, *Z.D.P.V.*, xxxviii (1915), pp. 249ff.; P. T. Cooke, *A.A.S.O.R.*, v (1923/4), pp. 105ff.; R. de Vaux and M. Stève, *Fouilles de Qiryat el-Enab*, Paris, 1951, pp. 10f. 'Azhar may preserve the name of Eleazar mentioned in 1 Sam. vii.1.
47. vi.21 – vii.2; cf. Ps. cxxxii.6 and 1 Chron. xiii.5f.; 2 Chron. i.4.
48. In 1 Sam. xiv.18 we read *'ēp̄ôḏ* for *'ᵃrôn* with Aquila, Symm. and most of the commentators. With the possible exception of Judges xx.27 the ark is never used for divination.
49. *Z.A.W.*, xlvii (1929), p. 184.
50. See for the earlier period Albright, *A.A.S.O.R.*, iv (1924), pp. 90ff., and Hertzberg, art. cit., pp. 61ff. An exhaustive summary can be found in J. Muilenburg (*St.Th.*), viii (1954), pp. 25ff., and in C. C. McCown, *Tell en-Naṣbeh*, I (1947), 3ff. The most recent treatment is that of D. Diringer, *Archaeology and Old Testament Study*, pp. 329–42.
51. Muilenburg, art. cit., pp. 37ff. For the Mizpah passages in 1 Sam. see pp. 98ff.
52. Alt dates this strand a generation after the fall of Jerusalem. See Muilenburg, art. cit., p. 30.

## NOTES TO CHAPTER II (pp. 14–27)

1. Gen. x.15; xv.19–21; Exod. iii.8, 17; xxiii.23; xxxiii.2; xxxiv.11; Deut. vii.1; xx.17; Joshua iii.10; ix.1; xi.3; xii.8; xxiv.11; Judges iii.5; 1 Kings ix.20; 1 Chron. i.13–16; 2 Chron. viii.7; Ezra ix.1; Neh. ix.8.

2. In Gen. xxxiv.2 and Joshua ix.7 LXX has 'Horite' for 'Hivite' but M.T. is supported by Aquila and Symm. in the former case and by many Greek MSS, Vetus Lat., Syr. and Eth. in the latter. In Joshua xi.3 the LXX reading 'Hittites', which was accepted by E. Meyer (*Die Israeliten und ihre Nachbarstämme*, Halle, 1906, pp. 334f.), has no textual support against M.T.
3. See preceding note.
4. E. Meyer, op. cit., pp. 328ff.; R. T. O'Callaghan, *Aram–Naharaim*, Rome, 1948, pp. 54f.; E. A. Speiser, *A.A.S.O.R.*, xiii (1933), pp. 27ff.; id., *Genesis*, Garden City, N.Y., 1964, pp. 282f.; W. F. Albright, *From the Stone Age to Christianity* (2nd edn), New York, 1957, pp. 152f., and many others.
5. *A.N.E.T.*, p. 378.
6. See most recently D. J. Wiseman, in *Archaeology and Old Testament Study*, pp. 118–35, with further bibliography.
7. B. Hrozný, *A.O.*, iv (1932), pp. 118ff.; *Syria*, xv (1934), pp. 144ff.; J. Gray, *Archaeology and Old Testament Study*, p. 154. For a criticism of some of Hrozný's conclusions see B. Landsberger, *J.C.S.*, viii (1954), pp. 56–60.
8. J. R. Kupper, *C.A.H.*, II, ch. I, pp. 16–26, 32–43; O'Callaghan, op. cit., p. 46; I. J. Gelb, *Hurrians and Subarians*, Chicago, 1944, pp. 64ff.; E. A. Speiser, *Cahiers d'Histoire Mondiale*, I (1953), 311ff.
9. On Megiddo see O'Callaghan, op. cit., p. 54; J. N. Schofield, *Archaeology and Old Testament Study*, pp. 309ff. B. S. J. Isserlin, *P.E.Q.*, lxxxviii (1956), pp. 141ff., suggests that the name Megiddo is Hurrian. On Taanach see A. Gustavs, *Z.D.P.V.*, l (1927), pp. 7ff.; W. F. Albright, *B.A.S.O.R.*, xciv (1944), pp. 12ff.; B. Maisler, *The Taanach Tablets*, in *Klausner Volume*, Tel Aviv, 1937, pp. 44–56. On Shechem: Gelb, op. cit., p. 59; O'Callaghan, op. cit., p. 65; Albright, *B.A.S.O.R.*, lxxxvi (1942), pp. 28ff., G. E. Wright, *Archaeology and Old Testament Study*, pp. 355ff. (with further bibliography).
10. Alt, *K.S.*, I, 98; P. Dhorme, *R.B.*, v (1908), pp. 500ff.; vi (1909), pp. 50ff., 368ff.; W. Riedel, *O.L.Z.*, xlii (1939), cols. 145–8; Albright, *C.A.H.*, II, ch. xx, pp. 3ff. Albright, p. 13, finds 61 non-Egyptian names in the letters of which 20 are Indo-aryan and 3 Hurrian. Despite his statement that no letter shows any evidence in Palestine for the kind of Hurrian substratum found further north, the name-analysis points to a situation typical in Mitanni since, in the nature of the case, the names of rulers would predominate.
11. Among earlier studies of the Hyksos we may cite Speiser, art. cit., pp. 48–51; Albright, *J.P.O.S.*, xv (1935), p. 228; Alt, *K.S.*, III, 1959 (1936), 44f.; R. M. Engberg, *The Hyksos Reconsidered*, Chicago, 1939; more recently Kupper, op. cit., pp. 37f., concludes that Syria played no part in the Hyksos movement and J. van Seters, *The Hyksos. A New Investigation*, New Haven, 1966, rules out any Hurrian participation.
12. The most recent study of these criteria is by de Vaux, *R.B.*, lxxv (1968), pp. 482–503.
13. Art. cit., pp. 486ff., especially pp. 496, 501f.
14. In particular with regard to the interpretation of the names Araunah (see *Les Livres de Samuel* (2nd edn), Paris, 1961, p. 251) and Ahiman, Sheshai and Talmai (*R.B.*, lv (1948), p. 327).
15. Albright, 'The Horites in Palestine', *From the Pyramids to Paul*, New York, 1935, pp. 21ff.; Speiser, *Genesis*, pp. 279ff.; *I.D.B.*, II, 645.
16. *A.A.S.O.R.*, xv (1935), p. 138; *The Other Side of the Jordan*, New Haven, 1940, pp. 33ff., 114ff.; *Rivers in the Desert*, London, 1959, pp. 153f.; *Explorations in Eastern Palestine*, III, New Haven, 1939. See also *The Biblical Archaeologist Reader*, New York, 1961, pp. 1–21.

17. See N. Glueck in *Archaeology and the Old Testament*, pp. 443f.; G. E. Wright, in *The Biblical Archaeologist Reader*, p. 14.
18. For Edomite associations with Kenizzites see Gen. xv.19; xxxvi. 10f., 42. The punning use of the word *qēn* (nest) in Num. xxiv.21 points to Edomite–Kenite connections. Kenites frequented the region settled by the Kenizzites Caleb and Othniel (Num. xxxii.12; Joshua xiv.6, 14; Judges i.13 etc.) and are thus associated both with Edomites and Judahites. See M. Noth, *The History of Israel* (2nd edn), London, 1960, pp. 56f., 76f.
19. With *Kenizzi*, *Perizzi* cf. *a-ki-iz-zi* king of Qatna during the time of Hurrian preponderance (Gustavs, *Z.D.P.V.*, l (1927), p. 14), *trgzz* from *tarḫu*, name of a Hurrian deity (H. L. Ginsberg and B. Maisler, *J.P.O.S.*, xiv (1934), p. 257) and *Perizzi*, name of a Hurrian envoy in an Amarna letter (J. A. Knudtzon, *Die El-Amarna-Tafeln*, Leipzig, 1915, p. 28). The three 'sons' of Anak are Ahiman, Sheshai and Talmai (Num. xiii.22; Joshua xv.14; Judges i.10). No Semitic origin is known for these names and the last resembles Hurrian *talma* (great). See W. Feiler, *Z.A.*, xlv (1939), pp. 225–7. It is also possible that -arba, component of the original name of Hebron (Kiriath-arba), is non-Semitic.
20. Hori (verse 22) – Hur (1 Chron. ii.50*b*); Shobal (verses 20, 29; 1 Chron. ii.50*b*); Ithran (verse 26) – Ithri (1 Chron. ii.53 – a Kiriath-jearim clan); Manahath (verse 23) – Manahathi (1 Chron. ii.54). We shall see later that the same overlap is attested for the Saulite names.
21. Reflected in the relations between Jacob and Esau (Gen. xxv.19ff. etc.) and the Yahwist's aetiological narrative about Cain and his descendants (Gen. iv). We have already discussed the Edomite and Israelite affinities of Kenites, Kenizzites and Manahathites.
22. *From the Pyramids to Paul*, p. 24. This suggestion is taken from Moritz, *Z.A.W.*, xliv (1926), p. 93.
23. For these texts see n. 2, p. 112.
24. *Z.A.W.*, xliv (1926), pp. 81ff.; *Le Muséon*, l (1937), pp. 101ff.
25. W. Feiler, *Z.A.*, xlv (1939), pp. 216ff.; H. L. Ginsberg and B. Maisler, *J.P.O.S.*, xiv (1934), pp. 243ff.; J. Lewy, *R.E.S.* (1938), pp. 49ff.
26. Close ethnic association between Arabs, the pre-Edomite population of Seir and Kenites is to be expected and is in fact attested in the Old Testament. For example, Kenites are living with Amalekites at the time of Saul (1 Sam. xv.6) and the family of the father of Moses' wife is both Kenite (Judges i.16) and Midianite (Exod. iii.1 etc.). A parallel case would be the names from el-Jîb, none of which antedates the seventh century, which are predominantly Yahwist.
27. Aiah (verse 24) cf. *aya* (god); Alvan (verse 23) cf. Hurrian names with the typical termination in *-wana* (Araunah may be derived from *ari-wana*, Feiler, art. cit., p. 225); Dishan and Dishon (verses 21, 25, 26) cf. *taišenni* (Feiler, art. cit., C. J. Gadd, *R.A.*, xxiii (1926), p. 81. Arisen of the Tusratta letter derives from *ari* (god) and *šenni* (brother); Kenaz (verses 11, 42) cognate with *kenizzi*, on which see n. 19 above; Shobal (verses 20, 29) cf. *šabil-iš*; Timna (verses 12, 22, 40) cf. *timnauš*, *tamnauš*. Far from proposing these as certain, we are simply saying that they have the same right to consideration as the Arabic derivations.
28. *Genesis*, pp. 279ff.; *I.D.B.*, II, 645.
29. *Genesis*, p. 264.
30. *Cahiers d'Histoire Mondiale*, 1/2 (1953), p. 30.
31. In Deut. ii.23 we are told that the Avvim were dispossessed by the Philistines. This occurs in a note which also refers to the dispossession of the Zamzummim

by Ammonites and of the Horites by Edomites; and it is significant that Anakim and Horites occur together with Avvim (Εὐαῖοι) in view of the Hurrian associations argued above. Speiser (*A.A.S.O.R.*, xiii (1933), p. 30) suggests comparison with a Hurrian personal name *ḫu(w)ya* and points to the Benjaminite place-name Avvim (Joshua xviii.23). We may note, finally, the Edomite place-name Avith (Gen. xxxvi.35) which LXX, strangely enough, translate as Gethaim (cf. Gittaim, 2 Sam. iv.3).

32. In a paper read before the Society of Biblical Literature, December 1966. In this paper, which Professor Mendenhall was kind enough to send me, he explicitly designates Que as the original homeland of the Gibeonites thus suggesting Luwian rather than Hurrian antecedents, though we should bear in mind that the population of Kizzuwadna was composed of both Luwian and Hurrian elements. Professor Mendenhall is currently assembling evidence for the widespread presence of groups of Anatolian provenance in Palestine and nearby regions down to and including the time of the arrival of the so-called Sea Peoples.
33. *A.N.E.T.*, pp. 279, 282–3.
34. E. O. Forrer, *P.E.Q.*, xlviii (1936), pp. 190ff. See also O. R. Gurney, *The Hittites* (2nd edn), Harmondsworth, 1954, pp. 59ff. The text is in *A.N.E.T.*, pp. 394–6.
35. See Aharoni, op. cit., pp. 158–60; *I.E.J.*, iii (1953), pp. 153ff.
36. See A. Malamat, *V.T.*, v (1955), pp. 1ff.; V. Korošec, *Hethitische Staatsverträge*, Leipzig, 1931, pp. 102ff.
37. See F. M. Abel, *Géographie de la Palestine*, II, 30f. He argues this even while identifying Benjaminite Mizpah with Tell en-Naṣbeh rather than with Nebi Samwil. Both Hivite centres had capital cities named Mizpah.
38. According to the Mursilis text the event would have taken place ca. 1350 B.C. The expansionist policy of Suppiluliumas may well have driven several groups, including Hurrians, into regions controlled by the Egyptians.
39. Hrozný, art. cit., pp. 121ff.; J. Heller, *A.O.*, xxx (1958), pp. 636ff. We cannot discuss conjectural associations between *'āḏām* and Edom or the representation of Cain as the *heros eponymos* of the Kenites.
40. O. Eissfeldt, *The Old Testament. An Introduction*, Oxford, 1966, p. 183; de Vaux, art. cit., p. 502. It may be noted that the parallel narratives of national disasters in 2 Sam. xxi.1–14 and xxiv.1–25 end respectively with *wayyē'āṯēr 'elōhîm lā'āreṣ* and *wayyē'āṯēr YHWH lā'āreṣ*, suggesting comparison with E and J in the Pentateuch (see p. 136, n. 35). For 'Amorite' as designating pre- or non-Israelite populations in general see in particular Gen. xv.16; Joshua xxiv.15, 18; Judges vi.10; 2 Kings xxi.11; Amos ii.9, 10. For the Amorites of history see K. Kenyon, *Amorites and Canaanites*, London, 1966.
41. H. Gunkel, *Genesis* (6th edn), Göttingen, 1964, p. 474; de Vaux, *La Genèse*, p. 210.
42. On Shechem see n. 9 above. The Shechem tablets from the beginning of the fourteenth century contain two Indo-aryan names: *šu-wa-ar-da-ta* and *bi-ra-še-n(a)*. The former occurs in the Amarna letters, the latter at Nuzi. We have seen that the names of the Anakim in pre-Israelite Hebron are almost certainly non-Semitic and one at least probably Hurrian (see Judges i.10). The term 'Hittite' in the texts referred to, as also in Ezek. xvi.3, is ethnic rather than political and may be taken to refer to or at least include a Hurrian element.
43. In addition to the Hurrian name (puti-ḫeba [Abdi-Ḫepat]) of the king of Jerusalem during the Amarna period we have the biblical names Uriah (2 Sam. xi.3 etc.) and Araunah (2 Sam. xxiv.16). Both Hittite (A. Gustavs,

*Z.A.W.*, xxxiii (1913), pp. 201ff.; O. Schröder, *Z.A.W.*, xxxv (1915), pp. 247ff.; A. H. Sayce, *J.T.S.*, xxix (1928), p. 401; M. Vieyra, *R.H.A.*, v (1938), pp. 113ff.) and Hurrian (W. Feiler, *Z.A.*, xlv (1939), p. 219) derivations have been suggested for the former. Albright compares Araunah with the Indo-aryan names Ariwana (*C.A.H.*, II, ch. xx, p. 14) which, however, Feiler (op. cit., p. 225) believes to be Hurrian (cf. Speiser, *A.A.S.O.R.*, xx, 1941, p. 218). A. H. Sayce (*J.T.S.*, xxii (1921), pp. 267f.) and H. B. Rosén (*V.T.*, v (1955), pp. 319f.) have proposed a Hittite origin for this name.

44. See pp. 47f., 76f.
45. At least half the more or less 3,000 personal names discovered at Nuzi are Hurrian and some of these belong to ḫabiru. See E. Chiera, *A.J.S.L.*, xlix (1933), p. 115; C. J. Mullo Weir, in *Archaeology and Old Testament Study*, pp. 73–86. For Syrian and Palestine cities see above, notes 8 and 9.
46. J. B. Pritchard, *Hebrew Inscriptions and Stamps from Gibeon*, Philadelphia, 1959.
47. Azariah (*'zryhw*), Amariah (*'mryhw*), Shebuel (*šb'l*), Hananiah (*ḥnnyhw*), Meshullam (*mšlm*).
48. Though see n. 43 on the name Uriah.
49. G. Bressan, *Samuele*, Turin, 1954, p. 497.
50. Feiler, art. cit., p. 221; Ginsberg and Maisler, art. cit., p. 257.
51. 2 Kings v. 18 refers to the temple of Rimmon at Damascus, cf. Rammânu the Assyrian storm-deity (*ramâmu* – roar cf. Hebrew *r'm* – thunder).
52. See Kupper, op. cit., p. 43.
53. Chiera, art. cit., pp. 117f. Hadad the Edomite is also mentioned in 1 Kings xi. 14.
54. P. Dhorme, in R. Dussaud (ed.), *Les Religions des Hittites et des Hourites*, Paris, 1945, pp. 336ff.
55. Another Hurrian storm-deity, Hamani, is attested at Alalakh (Wiseman, *Archaeology and the Old Testament*, p. 131) and possibly also at Ugarit (Hrozný, art. cit., p. 118).
56. See J. M. Myers, *I Chronicles*, Garden City, N.Y., 1965, with further bibliography.
57. Against Noth, *Z.D.P.V.*, lv (1932), pp. 97–124. Caleb is represented as husband to both Ephrath (verse 19) and Ephrathah (verse 24) who bear him respectively Hur and Ashhur. This is best understood as referring to the settlement of related groups in the same region.
58. See above notes 18 and 19.
59. E. Meyer, op. cit., p. 340; Ginsberg and Maisler, art. cit., p. 257.
60. We may note that Bezalel maker of the bronze altar which, according to the Chronicler (2 Chron. i. 5), was at Gibeon, is descended from the Hur whom we find often associated with Aaron in the Priestly document (Exod. xvii. 10 etc.).
61. See Gustavs, *Z.D.P.V.*, l (1927), p. 10.
62. Apart from Nadab son of Aaron, Amminadab (1 Chron. vi. 22) and Ahinadab (1 Kings iv. 14). Gibeon is one of four Benjaminite cities given to the descendants of Aaron (Joshua xxi. 17).
63. See pp. 5f.
64. Ahinoam, Ahimaaz (1 Sam. xiv. 50), Ahiezer (1 Chron. xii. 3), Ahijah, Ahitub (1 Sam. xiv. 3), Ahimelech (= Ahijah) (1 Sam. xxii. 9), Ahio (2 Sam. vi. 3), Ahishahar (1 Chron. vii. 10).
65. 1 Chron. viii. 19; Neh. xi. 9 (Benjaminites); Exod. vi. 21; 1 Chron. xxvi. 25 (Levites).

## NOTES TO CHAPTER III (pp. 28–40)

1. See M. Haran, *V.T.*, xi (1961), pp. 159ff., and on slavery and corvée labour in ancient Israel J. Mendelsohn, *B.A.S.O.R.*, lxxxv (1942), pp. 14ff.; clxvii (1962), pp. 31ff.
2. It does not occur in the Execration Texts, the Thutmoses III city-list or any of the inscriptions or tablets from the Amarna period. We cautioned earlier against too much reliance on an *argumentum e silentio* based on the excavations at el-Jîb. See Pritchard, *S.V.T.*, vii (1960), pp. 11f.
3. It also raises a problem with regard to their ready acceptance of servitude which may well be due, to some extent at least, to the late aetiological motif in Joshua ix, as will be suggested later in this chapter. For an imaginative but far-fetched explanation of this servile attitude see J. Craviotti, *Rev. Bibl.*, xxv (1963), pp. 137ff.
4. Letter 286 informs us that Abdi-ḫepa(t) was born in Jerusalem, see Knudtzon, op. cit., No. 286; S. A. B. Mercer, *The Tell El-Amarna Tablets*, II, Toronto, 1939, 706ff. That the Jebusites were basically Hurrian is proposed by Speiser, *Cahiers d'Histoire Mondiale*, 1/2 (1953), p. 321; A. Jirku, *Z.D.P.V.*, xliii (1920), pp. 58ff., *et al.* Albright, in *J.P.O.S.*, ii (1922), p. 127, took them to be of Cappadocian or Nesic descent.
5. Albright, *C.A.H.*, II, ch. xx, p. 9. The name also occurs in one of the Shechem tablets, on which see Albright, *B.A.S.O.R.*, lxxxvi (1942), pp. 28ff. The non-Israelite names (especially Talmai) in Num. xiii.22 may be taken to support Hebron as against Keilah for the location of Šuwardata's kingdom.
6. Based on I Chron. ii.50*b*ff. where Kiriath-jearim and Bethlehem are descended collaterally from Hur first-born of Ephrathah; the reference to 'the fields of Jaar' parallel with Ephrathah in Ps. cxxxii.6; the Bethlehemite Jaar (emended reading) in 2 Sam. xxi.19, and possibly also the reference to Ithrites in David's service (2 Sam. xxiii.38 cf. I Chron. ii.53). I have discussed these and other relevant texts at length in *J.B.L.*, lxxxvi (1969), pp. 143ff.
7. Assuming that Bit-Ninib is identical with Bethlehem. For the text see Mercer, op. cit., p. 722; *A.N.E.T.*, p. 489; Knudtzon, op. cit., 290, 15f.
8. See Mercer, op. cit., p. 722, and Dalman, op. cit., p. 224; Noth, *Z.D.P.V.*, lxv (1942), pp. 64ff.; Maisler, *J.P.O.S.*, x (1930), pp. 181ff.; A. Mallon, *J.P.O.S.*, viii (1928), pp. 1ff.; Jirku, *Z.D.P.V.*, xliii (1920), pp. 58ff.
9. The origins of Zadok have been the object of a great deal of research and speculation. For recent discussion see H. H. Rowley, *Worship in Ancient Israel*, London, 1967, p. 74 (bibliog. n. 4), and A. Cody, *A History of Old Testament Priesthood*, Rome, 1969, pp. 88–93.
10. C. C. Torrey (ed.), *The Lives of the Prophets*, Philadelphia, 1946, p. 30.
11. *The Biblical Period from Abraham to Ezra*, New York, 1963, p. 30. Noth, *The History of Israel*, p. 33, takes the view that the 'out-of-the-way position' of the Gibeonite cities explains why they do not appear in any of the letters, but it is difficult to suppose that the location of el-Jîb is really 'out-of-the-way'.
12. This view still holds the field and hardly requires exhaustive documentation. References in H. H. Rowley, *From Joseph to Joshua*, London, 1950; O. Eissfeldt, *C.A.H.*, II, ch. XXVI (*a*), Cambridge, 1965.
13. Though the Philistines arrived a century and a half later than the time we are speaking of they provide in some respects an instructive parallel to the Gibeonite cities. The Philistine pentapolis was clearly a political unity in some important respects though the individual cities enjoyed a degree of independence of action. Initially they did not have a monarchy but were

governed by *s^e^rānîm* (*tyrannoi*?). See Alt, *K.S.*, I, 113f.; B. D. Rahtjen, *J.N.E.S.*, xxiv (1965), pp. 100ff.; Noth, op. cit., p. 36. It may be noted that the Avvim (LXX Εὐαῖοι) are associated with the Philistines in Deut. ii.23 and Joshua xiii.3 in so far as they occupied the territory later conquered and settled by this branch of the Sea Peoples.

14. The flight of the Beerothites to Gittaim (2 Sam. iv.3) is best explained as the result of hostile action against the Gibeonite cities by Saul. Alt (*P.J.B.*, xxii (1926), p. 26, n. 4) and Noth (*Z.D.P.V.*, lv (1932), p. 117) explain the associations between Kiriath-jearim and groups located in Judah and particularly around Bethlehem (see n. 6 above) in the same way.
15. See p. 7.
16. Alt, *K.S.*, I, 110ff.
17. Alt, *K.S.*, I, 100, n. 1; *A.N.E.T.*, pp. 245ff.
18. At least during the Mitanni period, a chariot-aristocracy was one of the main features of Hurrian social organization. See Kupper, op. cit., p. 26; G. Conteneau, *S.D.B.*, iv (1949), cols. 128f.
19. Where names of kings appear in these chapters they are invariably different from those in the Amarna letters, see pp. 38f. We of course leave out of account the Amarna names *Yashuya* and *Benenima* which A. T. Olmstead (*The History of Palestine and Syria*, New York, 1931, pp. 197, 202) *et al.* confidently identified with Joshua and Benjaminites respectively. See Rowley, *From Joseph to Joshua*, p. 42; Alt, *K.S.*, I, 168, n. 3.
20. As did J. Garstang, *The Foundations of Biblical History: Joshua and Judges*, London, 1931, pp. 177f.
21. See especially Letters 249 and 287 and Albright, *C.A.H.*, II, ch. xx, pp. 10, 14.
22. Abdi-ḫepa(t) contains the name of a Hurrian goddess well known from other texts. Melchi-zedek, Adoni-zedek and Zadok are all associated with Jerusalem and are clearly theophoric. For Phoenician parallels to a deity *ṣdk* see Rowley, *Festschrift für Alfred Bertholet*, Tübingen, 1950, pp. 461ff. (the name occurs on pp. 464f.), and *J.B.L.*, lviii (1939), pp. 113ff.
23. For the principal attempts see K. Budde, *Z.A.W.*, vii (1887), pp. 136ff.; C. Steuernagel, *Das Deuteronomium und das Buch Josua* (2nd edn), Göttingen, 1923, pp. 241ff.; H. Holzinger, *Das Buch Josua*, Tübingen, 1901, pp. 30–2; S. R. Driver, *Introduction to the Literature of the Old Testament*, Oxford, 1913, p. 167; Eissfeldt, *Introduction*, pp. 251ff. Some (Budde, Wellhausen *et al.*) regard it as mainly J, others (Steuernagel, Procksch *et al.*) as mainly E, others again (Holzinger, Driver, Eissfeldt *et al.*) as a combination of both strands.
24. This is discussed in J. Blenkinsopp, *C.B.Q.*, xxviii (1966), pp. 207ff.
25. We may note that the angel of Yahweh (the ark?) departs from Gilgal, which is where the Gibeonite treaty was drawn up (Joshua ix.6). See K. Möhlenbrink, *Z.A.W.*, lvi (1938), p. 241. K. Galling (*Z.D.P.V.*, lxviii (1944/5), p. 30) believes that this incident is primarily associated with Bethel.
26. That Deut. xxvii represents a conflation of two traditions rooted in Shechem and Gilgal respectively is generally acknowledged. Moses and the elders speak in verse 1, Moses and the Levitical priests in verse 9, Moses alone in verse 11, the Levites alone in verse 14. Commands are given to set up stones immediately after crossing the Jordan, verse 2, and at Ebal, verse 4. The Levites are counted among the tribes at Gerizim, verse 12, they are cultic persons in verse 14. The command in verses 3–4 must refer to the same sanctuary as Joshua iv.19f. which speaks of stones set up near the Jordan at Gilgal. See Noth, *Das Buch Josua*, p. 33; A. Kuschke, *R.G.G.*, II (1958), 77f.; H. J. Kraus, *V.T.*, i (1951), pp. 194ff.

27. Sellin argued for a Gilgal sanctuary near Shechem (*Gilgal*, Leipzig, 1917, pp. 43f.) but Deut. xxvii and Joshua iv.19–24 clearly point to a sanctuary much nearer the Jordan. That Gilgal occurs in the Old Testament only twice without the article (Joshua v.9; xii.23) betrays the origin of the name in a local feature, probably a circle of stones (cf. Judges iii.19, the *pᵉsîlîm* near Gilgal).
28. J. Blenkinsopp, art. cit. We may note that Deut. ix.12 speaks of *entering into* the covenant not just renewing it, and in the same passage we hear of 'this sworn covenant' recalling the oath sworn by the elders in Joshua ix.15 (cf. 2 Sam. xxi.2).
29. 'Neither is it for us to put any man to death in Israel.' On this passage see H. Cazelles, *P.E.Q.*, lxxxvii (1955), p. 165.
30. If the original conclusion was '...to this day' (cf. v.9; vii.26; viii.29) the possibility must be considered that the Gibeonites served at the sanctuary of Gibeon after it was taken over by the Israelites and were later transferred to Jerusalem after the eclipse of 'the great high place'.
31. The term *'ēḏāh* occurs only in P. See B. Luther, *Z.A.W.*, lvi (1938), pp. 44ff.
32. Noth, *Das Buch Josua*, p. 55, and *Das System der Zwölf Stämme Israels*, Stuttgart, 1930, p. 102, n. 2 (apropos of Judges xx–xxi where *'ēḏāh* also occurs in a similar role).
33. They certainly were not asking for exemption from the principles of the Holy War on the grounds of their recent arrival in Canaan. The fact that they *had* arrived would have put them at once under the ban.
34. *Z.A.W.*, lvi (1938), pp. 241ff. According to Möhlenbrink, the latter strand referred originally to Shechem not Gibeon. This was suggested by A. Bruno, *Gibeon*, Leipzig, 1923, p. 135, but is not based on any evidence textual or otherwise.
35. *Das Buch Josua*, pp. 29ff.
36. *Die Bücher Josua, Richter, Ruth* (2nd edn), Göttingen, 1959, pp. 66–9.
37. *Le Livre de Josué* (2nd edn), Paris, 1958, pp. 57f.
38. For further references see J. Liver, *J.S.S.*, viii (1963), pp. 228f. Apart from a passing reference in Steuernagel, op. cit. (n. 23), p. 241, none of the commentators has made anything of the alternative use of *'îš yiśrā'ēl* and *bᵉnê yiśrā'ēl* as an indication of different sources. The use of these designations in Judges xix–xxi provides an instructive parallel, on which see E. Bertheau, *Das Buch der Richter und Ruth* (2nd edn), Leipzig, 1883, pp. 265, 269 (the first to draw attention to this); A. Besters, *E.T.L.*, xli (1965), pp. 34ff.
39. See p. 114, n. 14.
40. K. D. Schunck, *Benjamin*, Berlin, 1963, p. 23, finds support for the historicity of the treaty in the absence of any sign of burning or destruction from Late Bronze or Early Iron.
41. For documentation see D. McCarthy, *Treaty and Covenant*, Rome, 1963, pp. 52ff.; Noth, *Gesammelte Studien zum Alten Testament*, Munich, 1960, pp. 142ff.; H. W. Wolff, *V.T.*, vi (1956), p. 316 (the last two on a Mari treaty where the former term is used).
42. V. Korošec, *Hethitische Staatsverträge*, Leipzig, 1931; G. E. Mendenhall, *Law and Covenant in Israel and the Ancient Near East*, Pittsburgh, 1955; *B.A.*, xvii (1954), pp. 50ff.; F. C. Fensham, *B.A.*, xxvii (1964), pp. 96ff.; I. M. Grintz, *Zion*, xxvi (1960/1), pp. 69ff.; for the situation during the Amarna period see E. F. Campbell, *B.A.*, xxiii (1960), pp. 2–22.
43. We have examples from the hurrianized city of Alalakh of agreements sealed by an oath and a common meal. McCarthy, op. cit., pp. 57ff.; Fensham, art. cit., pp. 98f.

44. It is hardly possible to speculate who the deity may have been. In the Hittite-Egyptian treaty referred to in the Pestilence Prayer of Mursilis (see pp. 21f.) it is the Hurrian storm-god Teshub. According to J. Dus, *V.T.*, x (1960), pp. 353ff., Joshua x. 12 implies that ŠMŠ was a deity worshipped at Gibeon who guaranteed the treaty together with Yahweh. This hypothesis is examined in chapter IV.
45. On the curse in this type of treaty see McCarthy, op. cit., pp. 2, 28; Mendenhall, art. cit., pp. 50ff.; J. Scharbert, *Bib.*, xxxix (1958), pp. 5ff.; Fensham, *Z.A.W.*, lxxv (1963), pp. 155ff.
46. On the retribution clause see Korošec, op. cit., pp. 102ff.; A. Malamat, *V.T.*, v (1955), p. 8. Cf. the curses on Mati'el and his land in the Sefire treaty, McCarthy, op. cit., p. 62.
47. On the need for a written copy of a treaty see McCarthy, op. cit., pp. 4, 38. If the dating of the treaty suggested here is accepted this would be all the more cogent in view of the considerable time gap between the treaty and the reign of David. With respect to 2 Sam. xxi. 1 we note that 'to seek the face of Yahweh' suggests a visit to a sanctuary and, in view of the nature of the request, this would most naturally be the Gibeonite sanctuary as suggested by Hertzberg, *Die Samuelbücher* (2nd edn), Göttingen, 1960, p. 315, *et al.* In the Pestilence text Mursilis visits the sanctuaries of the gods to receive an oracle on the cause of the pestilence, *A.N.E.T.*, pp. 394f.
48. LXX reads 'Horite' but this does not oblige us to emend M.T.
49. See p. 112, n. 9.
50. This may be deduced from Gen. lxix. 5–7. See Speiser, *Genesis*, Garden City, N.Y., 1964, pp. 266ff. and other commentaries ad loc.
51. The parallelism would be closer still if, according to A. van den Born, *O.S.*, x (1954), pp. 201ff., Judges xix–xxi is interpreted as an anti-Saulite satire referring to his attack on the Gibeonites since in this case too the pretext for hostilities would be a sexual crime.
52. G. von Rad, *Genesis*, pp. 329f., contents himself with saying that it must have taken place considerably before 1200. Speiser, op. cit., p. 267, inclines towards the pre-Amarna period.
53. J. Bright, *A History of Israel*, Philadelphia, 1959, pp. 122–4; Rowley, *From Joseph to Joshua*, pp. 43f.; Albright, *C.A.H.*, II, ch. xx, p. 20.
54. D. N. Freedman and E. F. Campbell Jr (eds.), *The Biblical Archaeologist Reader*, II, New York, 1964, 264.
55. According to the most probable interpretation, though Aharoni, *The Land of the Bible*, pp. 161f., has recently argued for Gath in the Shephelah.
56. The archaeological evidence concerning the tribal territories of Benjamin and Ephraim, which concern us most closely here, has been presented thoroughly by Schunck, op. cit., pp. 18ff. Here and elsewhere, however, Schunck is not as cautious as the uncertain nature of the evidence demands.
57. Building on the work of earlier scholars, in particular that of Alt, Noth has stated this position very well in *The History of Israel*, pp. 68ff. The date of the entry of Benjamin in particular has been greatly confused by attempts to date the fall of Jericho on archaeological grounds. The results of the most recent excavations make it clear that this must be left out of account for the time being at least, see K. Kenyon, *Archaeology in the Holy Land* (2nd edn), London, 1965, p. 211.
58. Since it is unlikely that the biblical Benjaminites have any real connection with the *banû-yamina* of the Mari texts (Rowley, *From Joseph to Joshua*, pp. 115f.), the most probable hypothesis is that they acquired their name after the settlement and in consequence of their position to the south of the Joseph

tribes. Benjamin is therefore simply the 'southern province' of the Joseph tribes (Eissfeldt, *C.A.H.*, II, ch. XXXIV, p. 11).

59. This is further discussed on pp. 42ff.
60. Despite the military prowess of Benjamin as evidenced in Judges xx–xxi and Gen. xlix.27.
61. McCarthy, op. cit., p. 47, finds two biblical exceptions to this: the covenant between Abraham and Abimelech (Gen. xxi.22–4) and that between Yahweh and the fathers (Deut. vii.12). It is, however, not at all clear that Abraham is the superior in the first case, and in the second the juridical element is quite in the background.

## NOTES TO CHAPTER IV (pp. 41–52)

1. See p. 117, n. 23 and the discussion in Eissfeldt, *Introduction*, pp. 242–8.
2. *J.N.E.S.*, v (1946), pp. 105ff.
3. See especially Noth, *Das Buch Josua*, pp. 61f.; K. Elliger, *P.J.B.*, xxx (1934), pp. 47ff.
4. H. Gressmann, *Die Schriften des Alten Testaments*, Göttingen, 1922, p. 151; Sellin, *Gilgal, Ein Beitrag zur Geschichte der Einwanderung Israels in Palästina*, Leipzig, 1917, p. 43.
5. Eissfeldt, *C.A.H.*, II, ch. XXXIV, p. 10.
6. On the Deuteronomists' editing of Joshua see Eissfeldt, *Introduction*, pp. 255f.; E. Sellin–G. Fohrer, *Introduction to the Old Testament*, Nashville and New York, 1968 (E.Tr.), pp. 197, 202f.
7. The camp at Gilgal plays an important part in Joshua as a whole, but the Israelites would hardly have abandoned their newly won position in the Central Highlands. In verse 21 the camp is at Makkedah despite the fact that this city is not captured until later (verse 28). This inconsistency may be due to the insertion of the Makkedah episode.
8. Noth, op. cit., p. 61, points out this difficulty against Alt's *Heldensage* theory.
9. *K.S.*, I, 176ff.; B.Z.A.W., lxvi (1936), pp. 24f.
10. For the strategic importance of Beth-horon see J. Garstang, *The Foundations of Biblical History. Joshua and Judges*, London, 1931, p. 163. For the Amarna letters see Knudtzon, *Die El-Amarna-Tafeln*, p. 287 and for the biblical references *C.B.Q.*, xxvi (1964), pp. 429f.
11. Jerusalem (Joshua x.42; cf. Judges i.7f.), Hebron (Joshua x.3, 5, 36f.; cf. Judges i.10, 20), Debir (Joshua x.38; cf. Judges i.11).
12. See K. Budde, *Die Bücher Richter und Samuel, ihre Quellen und ihre Aufbau*, Freiburg, 1890, pp. 63ff.; G. F. Moore, *Judges* (I.C.C.), Edinburgh, 1895, p. 16; H. Holzinger, *Das Buch Josua*, Tübingen, 1901, p. 38; H. W. Hertzberg, *J.P.O.S.*, vi (1926), pp. 213ff.; H. M. Wiener, *J.P.O.S.*, ix (1929), p. 12, *et al.*
13. These difficulties are stressed by Alt, *K.S.*, I, 176ff., and Noth, op. cit., pp. 11ff., but rather underestimated by Wright, *J.N.E.S.*, v (1946), pp. 105ff.
14. See Noth, op. cit., pp. 60ff.; Schunck, op. cit., pp. 28ff.; Elliger, *P.J.B.*, xxx (1934), pp. 47ff.; A. Malamat, *The Conquest of Palestine in the Time of Joshua* (Hebrew) (2nd edn), Jerusalem, 1954, pp. 26f.
15. See Noth, op. cit., p. 63; Schunck, op. cit., p. 29, H. G. May, 'Joshua', in *Peake's Commentary on the Bible* (2nd edn), London, 1963, p. 297.
16. We should, however, add that this cannot be stated too categorically since the location of Makkedah is not known for certain; it may correspond to Khirbet el-Kheisun about fourteen miles west of Bethlehem. See J. Simons, *The Geographical and Topographical Lists of the Old Testament*,

Leiden, 1959, p. 273. Azekah is Tell Zakariya, about three miles south of Tell Rumeileh.

17. It can hardly be maintained that it is a later and highly coloured version of the sober prose account which precedes it.
18. Verse 13*a* is also dimetric. For a recent reconstruction of the original form see J. S. Holladay, *J.B.L.*, lxxxvii (1968), p. 168.
19. Verses 5, 8, 11, 13, 19, 22. *'āz* with imperfect also occurs in Exod. iv. 10; Isa. xli. 1; Mal. iii. 16; Ps. ii. 5; lxxxix. 20. See S. Mowinckel, *Z.A.W.*, liii (1935), pp. 130–2.
20. 1 Kings viii. 53*a* (LXX) = verse 13 (M.T.). ἐν βιβλίῳ τῆς ᾠδῆς presupposes *b^e sēper haššîr* and *šyr* may be a corruption by metathesis of *yšr*. This quotation is also introduced by *'āz*. The other quotation in the Old Testament from this collection is in 2 Sam. i. 17–27. See Eissfeldt, *Introduction*, pp. 132f., and S. Mowinckel, art. cit.
21. See Noth, op. cit., pp. 64f.; Hertzberg, *Die Bücher Josua, Richter, Ruth* (2nd edn), Göttingen, 1965, p. 74. B. J. Alfrink, *Studia Catholica*, xxiv (1949), pp. 238ff., places verses 12–14 after verse 42.
22. Holladay, art. cit., p. 168, thinks it is regular dimeter.
23. As recently by J. Dus, *V.T.*, x (1960), pp. 353ff., and J. Heller, *Comm. Viat.*, ix (1966), pp. 73ff.
24. Pointed out by Noth, op. cit., pp. 64f.; May, op. cit., p. 297, *et al.*
25. As in Heller, art. cit., p. 74. Holladay, art. cit., p. 169, argues persuasively against this view.
26. Even to enumerate them would take up more space than we can claim here. Holladay, art. cit., pp. 166–8, mentions some of the more recent and further references can be found in the standard commentaries. The interpretation offered below would exclude at once any alleged 'scientific' explanation as also those which presume poetic hyperbole or appeal to folklore motifs.
27. This translation is proposed by Alfrink, art. cit., p. 263, and J. Bright, *Interpreter's Bible*, II, New York and Nashville, 1953, 605.
28. 'to be silent' in Lev. x. 3; Jer. viii. 14; xlvii. 6; Lam. ii. 10; Ezek. xxiv. 17; Amos v. 13; Ps. iv. 4; xxx. 12; xxxi. 18; xxxv. 15; xxxvii. 7; lxii. 5; Job xxix. 21. 'to stand still' in Exod. xv. 16; 1 Sam. xiv. 9; Isa. xxiii. 3; Jer. viii. 14; Ps. cxxxi. 2; Job xxx. 27. Uncertain in 1 Sam. ii. 9; Jer. xxv. 27; xlviii. 2; xlix. 26; l. 30; li. 6; Lam. ii. 18; iii. 28.
29. G. R. Driver, *Canaanite Myths and Legends*, Edinburgh, 1956, p. 154. The meaning given is 'be quiet, still, silent'. See also his article, 'A confused Hebrew root', in *Sepher Tur-Sinai*, Jerusalem, 1960, pp. 1*–11*.
30. In the article referred to above, Holladay suggests a meaning on the basis of Mesopotamian hemerology and astronomy according to which the simultaneous appearance of sun and moon on a specific day would constitute a good omen. Apart, however, from the fact that the Old Testament has preserved no other request for an oracle of this kind, the apostrophe is here addressed *directly* to sun and moon. The parallel adduced below suggests an explanation much closer at hand.
31. The Holy War context of both passages makes this all the more significant. See Blenkinsopp, *C.B.Q.*, xxvi (1964), pp. 427ff.
32. See n. 23, together with Heller's earlier article, *A.O.*, xxx (1958), pp. 636ff.
33. According to Heller two deities, ŠMŠ and YRḤ.
34. For the invocation of deities in treaties of this kind see G. E. Mendenhall, *Law and Covenant in Israel and the Ancient Near East*, Pittsburgh, 1955; D. McCarthy, *Treaty and Covenant*, Rome, 1963. As Mendenhall points out (p. 34), in the Hittite treaties the gods of both the Hittites and the vassal are invoked.

35. J. B. Pritchard, *Hebrew Inscriptions and Stamps from Gibeon*, pp. 18ff.; *Gibeon where the Sun stood still*, p. 122 and fig. 82.
36. F. M. Cross, *B.A.S.O.R.*, clxviii (1962), pp. 12ff.; Pritchard, *The Bronze Age Cemetery at Gibeon*, Philadelphia, 1963, p. 154.
37. Beth-shemesh, En-shemesh, Ir-shemesh. In Judges i.35 Har-heres ('mountain of the sun') is a Danite city. Since it here occurs with Aijalon and Shaalbim which are listed with Beth-shemesh in 1 Kings iv.9 several scholars have identified it with Beth-shemesh, among whom Alt, *K.S.*, II, 86, Abel, *Géographie de la Palestine*, II, 282, 343, Aharoni, *The Land of the Bible*, pp. 216, 287; Mazar, *I.E.J.*, ii (1960), p. 67, rejects the identification but gives no reason. Though 'mountain of the sun' is not the same as 'temple of the sun', the close thematic relation between mountain and temple in the Ancient Near East might suggest an originally non-Hebrew name which has been handed down under two Hebrew forms.
38. Seal-impressions from the same mould have been unearthed at Beth-shemesh (Ain Shams) and Gibeon (el-Jîb) as noted by Pritchard, *Gibeon where the Sun stood still*, p. 118.
39. W. F. Albright, *A.J.S.L.*, liii (1936), pp. 1ff.; *B.A.S.O.R.*, lxxxiv (1941), pp. 7ff.; J. Gray, *J.N.E.S.*, viii (1949), pp. 27ff.; *The Legacy of Canaan* (2nd edn), Leiden, 1965, pp. 150, 179f.
40. See especially 2 Kings xxiii.11; Ezek. viii.16. Ps. xix and Ps. civ are also sometimes adduced as evidence and Dus, art. cit., p. 363, finds additional support in 1 Kings viii.12f. F. J. Hollis, in *Myth and Ritual*, ed. S. H. Hooke, London, 1933, and G. W. Ahlström, *Aspects of Syncretism in Israelite Religion*, Lund, 1963, p. 28, have no doubt that this was extensive.
41. 1 Sam. xxxi.10 and 1 Chron. x.10 read *tq'w*, which it is not necessary to emend as Köhler–Baumgartner do (*Lexicon in Veteris Testamenti Libros*, p. 398).
42. Art. cit., pp. 75f.
43. P. Dhorme, in R. Dussaud (ed.), *Les Religions des Hittites, et des Hourites, des Phéniciens et des Syriens*, *Mana* No. 1, Paris, 1945, pp. 335f.; O'Callaghan, op. cit., pp. 70f.; O. Gurney, *The Hittites* (2nd edn), Harmondsworth, 1954, pp. 139f.; J. Friedrich, *Z.A.*, xlix (1949), pp. 215ff., 225ff. (myths of the Hurrian sun-god).
44. Gurney, op. cit., p. 140.
45. Gurney, op. cit., p. 139; O'Callaghan, op. cit., p. 70.
46. For the text see Dhorme, *R.B.*, vi (1909), p. 53. For the Alalakh personal names see D. J. Wiseman, in *Archaeology and Old Testament Study*, p. 130, and the bibliography referred to by this author.
47. See in particular the treaties between Mursilis and Duppi-Teshub and between Suppiluliumas and Mattiwaza, *A.N.E.T.*, p. 205. The Aramaic treaty from Sefire is drawn up *qdm šmš wnr* (text and translation in J. A. Fitzmyer, *J.A.O.S.*, lxxxi (1961), pp. 178ff.
48. See H. Donner and W. Röllig, *Kanaanäische und Aramäische Inschriften*, II, Wiesbaden, 1964, 40 and *A.N.E.T.*, p. 499.
49. Donner and Röllig, op. cit., pp. 41f. The name is RŠP-ṢPRM.
50. In view of admittedly uncertain and fragmentary indications of ethnic affinity between the Gibeonites and early settlers in Edom we should note the similarity between the name of the Moabite king Balaq and that of the Edomite king Bela (*Bela'*). Even closer, however, is the similarity between *bil'ām ben-bᵉ'ôr* and *bela' ben-bᵉ'ôr*. This would not of course justify us in identifying these two persons; but it is entirely possible that in both cases there is a reference to *p'r* of the Karatepe inscription and *pa-ḫa-r(a)* of the Assyrian records. I must thank Professor G. E. Mendenhall for bringing this possibility to my attention.

51. As suggested by Heller, *A.O.*, xxx (1958), pp. 653f.; *Comm. Viat.*, ix (1966), p. 76. As far as I have been able to determine, there is no evidence either literary or iconographic for associating the Hurrian moon-god *Kušaḫ* with the deer thus providing, as alleged by Heller, an explanation of the moon in Aijalon (< *'ayyāl* = deer). In the absence of such evidence it is hardly sufficient to appeal to the figure of Artemis, goddess of the moon, who is often associated with the deer. We should, however, note that *Kušah,* the centre of whose cult was in Kizzuwatna, is generally associated with *Šimigi* the sun-god and is presented in treaty-texts as 'lord of the oath'. See E. Laroche, *R.H.R.*, cxlviii (1955), pp. 10ff.
52. For these and other motifs see G. von Rad, *Der heilige Krieg im alten Israel,* Zürich, 1951.
53. On this episode see J. Blenkinsopp, *C.B.Q.*, xxvi (1964), pp. 427ff.
54. Michmash is the modern Mukhmaš and Geba is Jeba.
55. With LXX[B] accepted by most commentators; see R. de Vaux, *Les Livres de Samuel* (2nd edn), Paris, 1961, p. 75, and J. Simons, op. cit., p. 316 (probable but not altogether certain).
56. This is surely not a reference to a tree-oracle, as proposed by Hertzberg, op. cit., p. 225.
57. The thunder is the voice of Yahweh, see Amos i.2; Joel iv.15–17 and the phrase *ytn ql* used in the Ugaritic texts of Baal (76 III 33; 51 V 70; 51 VII 29 in Gordon's enumeration).
58. *Die Bücher Samuelis und der Könige*, Nordlingen, 1887, ad loc.
59. This gives better sense topographically since M.T. speaks of two highways which 'go up' from Gibeah, one towards Bethel and the other towards Gibeah (sic).
60. See von Rad, op. cit., p. 28, n. 45.
61. Cf. Amos i.2 where the thunder proceeds from the sanctuary.

## NOTES TO CHAPTER V (pp. 53–64)

1. In Judges xx.45 Syr. reads 'Gibeon', but this reading has no further support.
2. In 1 Sam. xiv.18 read *'pwd* for *'rwn* with Aqu. and Symm. See H. P. Smith, *Samuel*, Edinburgh, 1904, p. 112; R. de Vaux, *Les Livres de Samuel*, p. 74, and most other commentators.
3. See pp. 78f.
4. Emendations are suggested by S. R. Driver, *Notes on the Hebrew Text and Topography of the Books of Samuel* (2nd edn), Oxford, 1913, p. 97; J. Wellhausen, *Der Text der Bücher Samuelis*, Göttingen, 1871, pp. 79ff.; K. Budde, *Die Bücher Samuel*, Tübingen, 1902, pp. 82f.; H. P. Smith, op. cit., p. 92. M. Noth, *Überlieferungsgeschichtliche Studien*, Halle, 1943, pp. 18ff., and *The History of Israel*, p. 176, wants to retain M.T.
5. Josephus, *Ant.* 6 14 9; Acts xiii.21.
6. In 1 Sam. xiii.14 Jonathan has already come of age and in xxxi.2 two younger sons fight at the battle of Gilboa.
7. Shamgar ben-Anath and Jerubbaal. Saul was initially supported by Samuel as Baraq was by Deborah.
8. Ishbaal (2 Sam. ii.8 etc.), Meribbaal (1 Chron. viii.34 cf. Mephibaal, 2 Sam. ix.2 etc. – his grandson). Names formed with -Mot are also found in his genealogy, 1 Chron. viii.36.
9. See O. Eissfeldt, *C.A.H.*, II, ch. XXXIV, pp. 34, 39; Schunck, op. cit., pp. 121ff.; H. Seebass, *Z.A.W.*, lxxix (1967), p. 168.

10. Albright, *A.A.S.O.R.*, iv (1922/3), p. 52; *Archaeology and the Religion of Israel*, pp. 103f.; Eissfeldt, op. cit., p. 35; H. Kjaer, *J.P.O.S.*, x (1930), pp. 87ff.
11. R. Kittel, *Geschichte des Volkes Israel* (6th edn), II, Stuttgart, 1925, 73, speaks of 'eine geräume Zeit'; Hertzberg, *Die Samuelbücher*, p. 50 and J. Morgenstern, *H.U.C.A.*, xvii (1942/3), p. 241, of about half a century.
12. *Das altisraelitische Ladeheiligtum*, Berlin, 1965, p. 48.
13. E.g. recently J. A. Soggin, *Z.A.W.*, lxxviii (1966), p. 183.
14. Op. cit., p. 191.
15. *A History of Israel*, pp. 165, 179.
16. The difference is very noticeable in passing from iv.1*a* to iv.1*b*, cf. the transition from Judges xiii.25 to xiv.1. See de Vaux, op. cit., p. 10; R. Press, *Z.A.W.*, lvi (1938), pp. 177ff.; Eissfeldt, *O.L.Z.*, xxx (1927), cols. 657ff.; xxxi (1928), cols. 801ff.
17. The ark of Yahweh (14 times), the ark of God (11 times), the ark of the God of Israel (6 times), the ark (twice), the ark of the covenant of Yahweh (twice, with variations).
18. We leave out of account 1 Sam. vii.13, the victory allegedly won by Samuel, which is historically unreliable and in fact contradicted by the subsequent narrative traditions.
19. Kittel, op. cit., p. 73 who describes the fate of the ark at this time as 'rätselhaft'; A. R. S. Kennedy, *1 and 2 Samuel*, Edinburgh, 1905, p. 218, says its neglect is 'inexplicable'; G. Little, *Interpreter's Bible*, II, New York and Nashville, 1953, 1076, states that so far no satisfactory answer has been given to this problem.
20. Saul's intemperate policy may have driven them, as it did David, into the arms of the Philistines. See H. Cazelles, *P.E.Q.*, lxxxvii (1955), p. 170.
21. There is much to support the view, first proposed and elaborated by Reichel, Dibelius and Gunkel, that the ark was originally an empty throne. For more recent literature see R. de Vaux, *Ancient Israel*, London, 1961, p. 300; G. von Rad, *Old Testament Theology* I, 23; Alt, *K.S.*, I, 345ff.; K. H. Bernhardt, *Das Problem der altorientalischen Königsideologie im Alten Testament*, Leiden, 1961, p. 99; Eissfeldt, *RGG*, VI, 1875f.
22. A. van den Born, *O.S.*, x (1954), pp. 201ff.
23. For significant comments on this aspect of the narrative see J. Muilenburg, in *Tell en-Naṣbeh* (ed. C. C. McCown), I, New Haven, 1947, 45f.; O. Eissfeldt, *Kleine Schriften*, II, Tübingen, 1963, 70; Schunk, op cit., p. 63; A. Besters, *E.T.L.*, xli (1965), pp. 29, 32. For the editorial history of the narrative see O. Eissfeldt, pp. 65ff.; Schunck, pp. 57f.; C. Kuhl, *Die Entstehung des Alten Testaments*, Berne, 1953, pp. 129f.
24. See J. Muilenburg, *J.B.L.*, lxxv (1956), pp. 194ff.; J. A. Soggin, *V.T.*, xi (1961), pp. 432ff.; R. Brinker, *The Influence of Sanctuaries in Early Israel*, Manchester, 1946, pp. 145f.
25. If instead of the problematic *hmryh* of M.T. we read with Syr. *h'mry* we may even suggest a connection between the attempted ritual sacrifice of Isaac and that of the Saulites, as do E. Sellin, *Gilgal*, Leipzig, 1917, p. 76 and H. W. Hertzberg, *Z.A.W.*, xlvii (1929), p. 191. The Gibeonites are described as Amorites (2 Sam. xxi.2), the term 'the mountain of Yahweh' occurs only in 2 Sam. xxi.6 and Gen. xxii.14 with the exception of Num. x.33 which deals with the ark, and *bhr YHWH yr'h* (Gen. xxii.14) may be compared with *bgb'wn nr'h YHWH* (1 Kings iii.5).
26. See J. Gray, *I and II Kings*, London, 1963, pp. 116ff.; H. Cazelles, *S.V.T.*, iii, (1955), pp. 26ff.
27. Hos. ix.9 and x.9 refer indirectly to Saul. The opposition between Samuel

and Saul is seen most clearly in 1 Sam. viii.10–22; xiii.8–15 and xv.10–31.

28. Noth, *Überlieferungsgeschichtliche Studien* I, Halle, 1943, 54; C. A. Simpson, *J.S.S.*, iii (1958), p. 395.

29. See Eissfeldt, *C.A.H.*, II, ch. XXXIV, p. 40 and above p. 117, n. 14.

30. Located at Tell el-Fûl. See Albright, *A.A.S.O.R.*, iv (1922/3), pp. 1ff.; *B.A.S.O.R.*, lii (1933) pp. 6ff.; L. Sinclair, *B.A.*, xxvii (1964), pp. 52ff.; *A.A.S.O.R.*, xxxiv (1954/5), pp. 10ff.; K. Kenyon, *Archaeology in the Holy Land* (2nd edn), London, 1965, pp. 237ff.

31. Noth, *Das Buch Josua*, p. 113; Alt, *K.S.*, II, 31; de Vaux, *Les Livres de Samuel*, p. 234. For a discussion with recent bibliography see Schunck, op. cit., pp. 89, 118f. H. P. Smith, op. cit., p. 69, conjectures that M.T. may have contained a reference to Zela where Saul's family was buried.

32. D. R. Ap-Thomas, *V.T.*, xi (1961), pp. 241ff., argues that *dōd* (1 Sam. x.14) means 'one who takes the place of a father' or 'deputy', 'governor' and refers to the Philistine garrison-commander to whom Saul had to report and from whom, naturally, he withheld the information about his kingship. There is some discrepancy between 1 Sam. xiv.49–51 and 1 Chron. viii.33 as to the exact relationship between Saul, Ner and Abner.

33. Saul, Aiah, Jeush, Ishmael, Hanan, Matri (cf. Matred, Gen. xxxvi. 39). The similarity between these last two amounts to identity in 1 Sam. x.21 (LXX$^{A}$): Ματταρειτ.

34. See p. 113, n. 20.

35. For example, Maacah, the region in northern Transjordania usually mentioned with Geshur (Joshua xiii.11; xii.5 etc.). According to 2 Sam. iii.3, David married Maacah daughter of Talmai king of Geshur which explains why Absalom fled to Geshur (2 Sam. xiii.37). According to the Chronicler's genealogy Maacah is associated with the Calebite clan (1 Chron. ii.48) and is the 'mother' of Gibeon (viii. 29; ix.35) while Talmai is the name of a pre-Israelite group near Hebron (Judges i.10; Joshua xv.14) which is, as we have seen, probably of Hurrian derivation. See B. Mazar, *J.B.L.*, lxxx (1961), pp. 16ff.

36. It has often been suggested that 1 Sam. i.20 (cf. verses 27–8) referred originally to Saul not Samuel and that *šā'ûl* is a technical term referring to the vow rather than a personal name; see commentaries ad loc. and M. Noth, *Die israelitische Personennamen im Rahmen der gemeinsemitischen Namengebung*, Stuttgart, 1926, p. 136. The other occurrences of the personal name are enought to render the latter hypothesis unconvincing. The absence of the theophoric element certainly seems to call for comment, and we cannot discount the possibility that a non-Israelite name has been given a form which makes it susceptible of a more orthodox meaning. A type of personal name formed with *pal-* (from the verb meaning 'to ask for') exists in Hurrian, e.g. *pa-al-ti* in the Nuzi tablets (E. Chiera, art. cit., p. 117) with which we may compare Palti (Paltiel) husband of Michal Saul's daughter.

37. See p. 113, n. 24 and J. R. Bartlett, *J.T.S.*, N.S. xvi (1965), p. 308.

38. *Z.D.M.G.*, xl (1886), pp. 166f.

39. For the Edomite name Qaushgabri see *A.N.E.T.*, pp. 291, 294; Qausanal is known from excavations at Elath; N. Glueck, *Rivers in the Desert: A History of the Negev*, New York, 1960, pp. 165f., 168. See also J. Wellhausen, *Reste Arabischen Heidentums* (2nd edn), Berlin, 1897, p. 67. Noth, op. cit., p. 171, n. 3, suggested an Akkadian cognate and we may add that a Hurrian name *ki-iš* occurs in the Nuzi tablets; see Chiera, art. cit., p. 117.

40. Saul (?), Kish, Ner, Matri, Merab, Michal, Palti, Aiah, Rizpah, Pithon, Tarea, Pelet.

41. J. B. Pritchard, *Hebrew Inscriptions and Stamps from Gibeon*, pp. 11, 22f.
42. C. Gordon, *Ugaritic Textbook*, Rome, 1965, p. 447; F. Thureau-Dangin, *Syria*, xii (1931), pp. 234 ff.; xv (1934), pp. 137ff.
43. H. Donner and W. Röllig, *Kanaanäische und Aramäische Inschriften*, II, Wiesbaden, 1964, 239, 245, for translation and comment on the context. Also J. Fitzmyer, *J.A.O.S.*, lxxxi (1961), p. 191.
44. M.T. Ishbosheth cf. 1 Chron. viii. 33; ix. 39. If we accept Albright's suggested derivation from *'eš ba'al* (*Archaeology and the Religion of Israel* (4th edn), Baltimore, 1956, p. 113) the polemical intent behind the name becomes apparent.
45. The story of Bath-shua's sons in Gen. xxxviii. 2ff. is concerned with the fratriarchate and levirate, customs which appear to be of Hurrian origin; see Albright, in *From the Pyramids to Paul* (ed. Leary), New York, 1935, p. 18; P. Koschaker, *Z.A.*, xli (1933), pp. 1ff.; C. H. Gordon, *B.A.*, iii (1940), pp. 1–12.
46. See above n. 36 and R. H. Pfeiffer and E. A. Speiser, *A.A.S.O.R.*, xvi (1935/6), p. 159. Pal-teshub also occurs in these texts. In Gen. xxxvi. 24 = 1 Chron. i. 40 Aiah is son of Zibeon the Horite. The name is practically identical with Hurrian *aya* ('god'). See W. Feiler, *Z.A.*, xlv (1939), p. 219; Ginsberg and Maisler (Mazar), *J.P.O.S.*, xiv (1934), p. 257.
47. Gen. xxxvi. 37–9. The date of the king-list depends on the interpretation of verse 31 which refers either to the time of Saul or, more probably, of David (see H. Gunkel, *Genesis* (6th edn), Göttingen, 1964, pp. 393f.; G. von Rad, *Genesis*, London, 1961, pp. 339ff.). Since each king reigns in a different place and there is no father–son succession it is often proposed that the list is of dynasts roughly contemporary with each other, not unlike the Israelite 'judges' (Speiser, *Genesis*, p. 282; B. Moritz, *Le Muséon*, I, 1937, 101ff.; Bartlett, art. cit., pp. 301ff.). If this is so, they may still be roughly contemporary with Saul, but one cannot dispel the suspicion that *taḥaṯ* implies temporal succession. In this case we must note that the Edomite Saul is antepenultimate. If the last king Hadar (Hadad?) was contemporary with David, the Edomite Saul would have flourished either shortly before or at the same time as the Israelite Saul. Honeyman, *J.B.L.*, lxvii (1948), pp. 23f., actually identifies the two as he does Baal-hanan with David whose personal name was El-hanan (2 Sam. xxi. 19). Moritz, art. cit., p. 102, dates the series ca. 1200–1040 and Albright (*Archaeology and the Religion of Israel*, p. 206, n. 58) dates Hadar (= Hadad II) contemporary with David. The reference to *'allûpîm* in early Edom suggests a passage from a non-monarchical to monarchical government similar to what happened in Geshur (B. Mazar, *J.B.L.*, lxxx (1961), p. 20), in Shechem at the time of Abimelech and in Gibeon at the time of Saul.
48. In 1 Sam. xxii. 9 he is described as *niṣṣāb 'al 'aḇḏê šā'ûl* which would most naturally mean 'placed over' Saul's officials, especially in view of xxi. 8 (*'abbîr hārō'îm 'ašer lᵉšā'ûl*). This latter description may also imply a cultic office by analogy with *nqd* in the Ugaritic texts and perhaps also in the Old Testament (see A. S. Kapelrud, *Central Ideas in Amos*, Oslo, 1961, pp. 5ff.).
49. Use of the term *ḥeseḏ* in this text, as well as other indications, may imply a treaty existed between early Israelites and Kenites. See F. C. Fensham, *B.A.S.O.R.*, clxxv (1964), pp. 51–4.
50. 1 Sam. xxxi. 11–13. Cremation was decidedly not an Israelite custom.
51. See D. R. Hillers, *B.A.S.O.R.*, clxxvi (1964), pp. 46f.
52. See Mazar, art. cit., p. 23. For Talmai see n. 35 above.
53. It may be added that according to 1 Sam. xxv. 44 Saul gave his daughter Michal in marriage to Palti son of Laish of Gallim. The place-name is otherwise not attested but Laish suggests a location in the extreme north of Palestine

(Judges xviii. 7). It seems reasonable to assume the settlement in these regions of Anatolian and/or Hurrian elements. The origins of David's family, in some respects equally problematic, cannot be discussed here.

54. As is generally recognized, the representation of Samuel as 'judge' is secondary and that such a victory took place at this time is flatly contradicted by the subsequent course of events. On this passage see pp. 78f.

55. See p. 59. It is possible that the Gibeonite cities had been under Philistine control for some time prior to the events narrated in 1 Sam. For the earliest evidence to date of Philistine presence in Palestine see G. E. Wright, *B.A.*, xxix (1966), pp. 70ff.

56. They may have claimed legal suzerainty over Palestine as proposed by Alt, *K.S.*, II, 3f., and Eissfeldt, *C.A.H.*, p. 35. Wright, art. cit., p. 72, states that they were settled there in garrisons by Ramses III (†1144). In any case, it seems that the Philistine garrison system is modelled on that of the Egyptians during the Amarna age (see Alt, *K.S.*, I, 113ff.).

57. The clearest evidence for their pacification policy is in 1 Sam. xiii. 19–21.

58. *'iḇrîm* occurs eight times in 1 Sam. Of these occurrences six are in the mouth of the Philistines (iv. 6, 9; xiii. 19; xiv. 11; xxix. 3; xiii. 3 reading 'when the Philistines heard that the *'iḇrîm* had revolted . . .'). xiii. 7 (M.T.) refers to *'iḇrîm* fleeing across the Jordan and xiv. 21 clearly distinguishes *'iḇrîm* from Israelites. Hence the two terms are not simply convertible; Israelites belong to a group or class described as *'iḇrîm*.

59. Isa. x. 32 and Neh. xi. 32 suggest a location near Anathoth and Jerusalem which conflicts with Jerome's location at Nobe (now 'Annabe) near Lydda (*Ep.* 108 and Abel, *Géographie de la Palestine*, II, 400). Various sites near Jerusalem have been suggested: Raš el-Mešārif, Raš umm et-Tala' on the eastern slope of Mt. Scopus, Qu'meh about a mile to the north. Nob has roughly the same meaning as Scopus (*skopos*), which may not be coincidental. At all events a location in this area has the advantage of placing Nob near Saul's city Gibeah (see 1 Sam. xx. 6f.) identified with Tell el-Fûl. On this question see E. E. Voigt, *J.P.O.S.*, iii (1923), pp. 79ff.; A. Alt, *P.J.B.*, xxi (1925), pp. 12f.; Simons, op. cit., p. 319.

60. M.T. reads 'Beth-aven' which we emend with $LXX^{L}$ and Vetus Lat. See Smith, op. cit., p. 113.

61. This last is suggested by H. Cazelles, *P.E.Q.*, lxxxvii (1955), p. 170.

62. Schunck, op. cit., pp. 132f. who refers to I. Hylander, *Der literarische Samuel–Saul Komplex*, 1932, p. 262.

63. See pp. 95ff.

64. See p. 88.

65. Schunk, op. cit., pp. 131ff. The city was enlarged during the Iron Age (see Pritchard, *V.T.*, vii (1960), pp. 9f.) but this cannot be associated necessarily with the period of Saul's ascendancy.

66. M.T. reads 'Geba' which we emend with LXX and 1 Chron. xiv. 16 supported by Isa. xxviii. 21. $LXX^{B}$ reads 'from Gibeon to the land of Gazera', $LXX^{A}$ 'from Gibeon to Gaza' and Vulg. 'de Gabaa usquedum venias Gezer'.

1. For this title in 1 Sam. i.3 and iv. 4 see B. Wambacq, *L'Épithète divine Jahvé Ṣeba'ôt*, Bruges, 1947; Alt, *K.S.*, I, 345ff.; O. Eissfeldt, *R.G.G.*, VI, cols. 1875f.; id., *Misc. Acad. Berol.*, II/2 (1950), pp. 135ff.; V. Maag, in *Köhler Festschrift*, 1950, pp. 27ff.; R. Smend, *Jahwekrieg und Stämmebund*, Göttingen, 1963, pp. 59ff.; de Vaux, *Ancient Israel*, London, 1961, p. 304.
2. See pp. 104ff.
3. 1 Sam. xiv.3, cf. xxi.2; xxii.9. The change from Ahijah to Ahimelech may be due to association with the ark-kingship of Yahweh. Another Ahijah from Shiloh is mentioned in 1 Kings xi.29ff.
4. Early references to the twelve-tribal idea take us back either to Shiloh or to an early Benjaminite sanctuary: the tearing of Ahijah's cloak into twelve parts (1 Kings xi.29ff.), the twelvefold dismembering of the concubine after the crime of the men of Gibeah (Judges xix.29; cf. 1 Sam. xi.7), the Gilgal *dodekalithon* tradition (Joshua iii.12; iv. 1–24; Deut. xxvii.2–3). On this question see M. Noth, *Das System der Zwölf Stämme Israels*, Stuttgart, 1930; Eissfeldt, *C.A.H.*, II, ch. XXXIV, p. 16; A. Caquet, *Sem.*, xi (1961), pp. 17ff.; H. J. Kraus, *Worship in Israel*, Oxford, 1966, pp. 161–5. If the ark was moved from Gilgal to Shiloh (Kraus, p. 177) Benjaminite influence on the Shiloh cult would be readily understandable. E. Nielsen, *S.V.T.*, vii (1960), pp. 61ff., points out further associative links between Shiloh and Benjamin.
5. This is denied by W. R. Arnold, *Ephod and Ark*, Cambridge, Mass., 1917, but his arguments are vitiated by arbitrary textual emendation.
6. On the location of Nob see p. 127, n. 59. That the Nob of 1 Sam. xxi–xxii was an ark-sanctuary is accepted, *inter alios*, by Albright, *Archaeology and the Religion of Israel*, p. 104; S. H. Hooke, in *Peake's Commentary on the Bible* (2nd end.), London and Edinburgh, 1962, p. 145.
7. A. Schlatter, *Zur Topographie und Geschichte Palästinas*, Stuttgart, 1893, pp. 246ff.; H. A. Poels, *Le Sanctuaire de Kirjath-Jearim. Étude sur le lieu du culte chez les Israélites au temps de Samuel*, Louvain, 1894; T. K. Cheyne, *E.B.*, iii (1902), col. 3430; A. Bruno, *Gibeon*, Leipzig, 1923, pp. 69ff.; Hertzberg, *Z.A.W.*, xlvii (1929), pp. 177ff.; I. Hylander, *Der literarische Samuel–Saul Komplex*, Uppsala, 1932, pp. 286, 291f. Hertzberg (art. cit. and *Die Samuelbücher*, pp. 144f.) ingeniously but unconvincingly defends the same view on the grounds that the tent in which David placed Goliath's armour is the Nob sanctuary where the same giant's sword was kept and, at the same time, the tent-sanctuary located by the Chronicler at Gibeon.
8. See L. Köhler and W. Baumgartner, *Lexicon in Veteris Testamenti Libros*, Leiden, 1951, p. 587 (*sub voce neḇô*).
9. Num. xxxii.3, 38; xxxiii.47; Isa. xv.2; Jer. xlviii.1, 22; 1 Chron. v.8; Moabite Stone, line 14. The form in this last is *nbh* as in 1 Sam. xxi.1. There was another Nebo in Judah, Ezra ii.29; x.43; Neh. vii. 33. In view of the ethnic associations pointed out earlier between populations around Gibeon and in Transjordan we may note the occurrence in the Moabite inscription of Hauronen (*ḥwrnn*, line 31) identical with Horonaim, cf. the two Beth-horons near Gibeon, and Qaryathen (*qrytn*, line 10) identical with Kiriathaim. Mazar and Aharoni state that a Kiriathaim features in the list of cities which Sheshonk claimed to have captured and that this city must be identified with Kiriath-jearim; see p. 111, n. 45. The name of Mesha's father *kmšyt*, supplied from another Dìbon fragment recently discovered, is compared by D. N. Freedman, *B.A.S.O.R.*, clxxv (1964), pp. 50f., with the name Yetheth an Edomite chief in Gen. xxxvi. 40.

10. See Judges xxi. 19ff.; I Sam. ii. 12–17, 22–5, 27–36; iii. 12–14. Also Kraus, op. cit., pp. 173–8.
11. For the cultic interpretation of *'abbîr hārō'îm* see p. 126, n. 48 and cf. the description of (some) Gibeonites as 'hewers of wood and drawers of water' which may imply a function necessary for the carrying out of ritual including sacrificial ritual. This is, of course, hypothetical. It may be added that the *nbh* of the Mesha inscription was also a cultic centre reading *'t kly YHWH* (lines 17f.).
12. That Jerusalem rather than Gibeon became his capital and thus achieved the enormous prestige which it has may be due to the historical accident that Jerusalem was captured by him before Gibeon.
13. J. Wellhausen, *Prolegomena zur Geschichte Israels* (6th edn), Berlin, 1905, pp. 17ff. More recently A. Besters, *E.T.L.*, xli (1965), pp. 20ff.; W. H. Irwin, *R.B.*, lxxii (1965), pp. 161ff.; Rowley, *Worship in Ancient Israel*, London, 1967, pp. 58ff.
14. Alt, *K.S.*, I, 1ff.; II, 7ff.; Noth, *Das System der zwölf Stämme Israels*, pp. 86ff. Also de Vaux, *Ancient Israel*, pp. 302 ff.
15. For the importance of the ark in the pre-monarchical period see G. von Rad, *Old Testament Theology* I, London and Edinburgh, also New York, 1962, 17ff.; Noth, *The History of Israel*, pp. 90ff.; H. J. Kraus, *Worship in Israel*, Oxford, 1966, pp. 126f. Dus's theory (*T.Z.*, xvii (1961), pp. 1ff.; *V.T.*, xiii (1963), pp. 126ff.) that the ark-sanctuary changed every seven years, built on an original interpretation of I Sam. vi. 7ff., is too subjective to be convincing.
16. According to some scholars, e.g. Kraus, *Worship in Israel*, pp. 176f., this must have taken place at Gilgal. E. Nielsen, *Shechem. A Traditio-Historical Investigation*, Copenhagen, 1959, p. 317; *S.V.T.*, vii (1960), pp. 63f., points out some interesting connections between the Shiloh sanctuary and the tribe of Benjamin though one would like to know on what grounds he claims Samuel to be Benjaminite.
17. According to Sellin, *Gilgal*, pp. 49, 91, and *Das Zelt Jahwes*, Leipzig, 1913, p. 187, Gibeon was a tent-sanctuary even before Shiloh. E. Auerbach, *Wüste und gelobtes Land*, I, Berlin, 1932, 90ff., claims that it was the first Israelite sanctuary established in Canaan.
18. This is accepted by Kittel, *Geschichte des Volkes Israel*, I, 430ff.; H. Gressmann, *Die Anfänge Israels* (2nd edn), Göttingen, 1922, p. 152; Hertzberg, *Z.A.W.*, xlvii (1929), pp. 176f.; Pritchard, *S.V.T.*, vii (1960), p. 3; M. Haran, *V.T.*, xi (1961), p. 161, *et al.*
19. H. S. Nyberg, *Arch. für Rel.*, xxxv (1938), pp. 368ff.; I. Engnell, *Svensk Bibl. Upp.*, II, cols. 1115f.; E. Nielsen, op. cit., p. 271, n. 2; Ahlström, op. cit., p. 9 are all convinced that *'lw* in I Sam. ii. 10 refers to a deity worshipped in Shiloh and identical with *'elyōn*. Nyberg, art. cit., pp. 372f., finds the same deity in Deut. xxxiii. 12 by reading: *yᵉḏîḏ YHWH yiškōn lāḇeṭaḥ* / *'alû ḥōp̄ēp̄ 'ālāw kol-hayyôm* – "Alû covereth him all the day long'. However we evaluate this ingenious emendation we cannot conclude that the sanctuary in question was Shiloh unless we arbitrarily suppose, with Schunck, op. cit., pp. 70ff., *et al.*, that this verse belongs to the Joseph oracle.
20. Recent scholarship generally admits the antiquity of the collection as a whole, e.g. Eissfeldt, *The Old Testament. An Introduction*, pp. 227–9; Schunck, op. cit., pp. 70–2; F. M. Cross and D. N. Freedman, *J.B.L.*, lxvii (1948), pp. 191ff. We may presume that some at least of the individual sayings are older than the collection as a whole.
21. A. Schlatter, *Zur Topographie und Geschichte Palästinas*, Stuttgart, 1893, pp. 246ff. Albright, *A.A.S.O.R.*, iv (1922–3), p. 40, attributes the same view to Lepsius but I have been unable to consult his work *Reich Christi* published in 1903.

22. A. van Hoonacker, *Le Lieu de Culte dans la législation rituelle des Hébreux*, Ghent, 1894; A. Poels, *Le Sanctuaire de Kirjath-Jearim*, Louvain, 1894; id., *Examen critique de l'Histoire du sanctuaire de l'arche*, Louvain, 1897.
23. See reviews in *R.B.*, iv (1895), pp. 97ff. (J. P. van Kasteren); *R.B.*, vi (1897), p. 630 (M. J. Lagrange); *Theol. Tijdschrift*, xxx (1896), pp. 200ff. (W. H. Kosters), and critical remarks by L. H. Vincent, *R.B.*, xxxi (1922), p. 374, and A. Besters, art. cit., pp. 21f.
24. Vincent, art. cit., p. 374.
25. *Gibeon*, Leipzig, 1923.
26. *Z.A.W.*, xlvii (1929), pp. 161ff. In *Die Samuelbücher*, p. 315, n. 2, he correctly describes Bruno's work as containing 'viel Phantastisches'.
27. W. H. Kosters, *Theol. Tijdschrift*, xxvii (1893), pp. 361ff.
28. R. Brinker, *The Influence of Sanctuaries in Early Israel*, Manchester, 1946, p. 160.
29. *O.S.*, x (1954), pp. 201ff.
30. This is widely admitted by the commentators; see Bleek–Wellhausen, *Einleitung in das Alte Testament* (4th edn), Berlin, 1874, pp. 208ff.; J. Wellhausen, *Die Composition des Hexateuchs und der historischen Bücher des Alten Testaments*, Berlin, 1889, p. 240; Thenius–Löhr, *Die Bücher Samuelis* (3rd edn), Leipzig, 1893, ad loc.; W. Nowack, *Richter, Ruth und Bücher Samuelis*, Göttingen, 1902, pp. xvii, xx, xxxiff.; K. Budde, *Die Bücher Samuel*, Tübingen, 1902, p. 32; Eissfeldt, *The Old Testament. An Introduction*, pp. 269ff., *et al.*
31. E.g. Budde, op. cit., p. 32; Nowack, op. cit., p. xvii; C. H. Cornill, *Zur Quellenkritik der Bücher Samuel*, Königsberg, 1887, pp. 25ff. Source-division based on titles for the ark (*'ᵃrôn YHWH*, *'ᵃrôn 'elōhîm*), as in Budde, op. cit., p. 226, is not a safe criterion either in view of the long and complicated history behind these traditions where the titles occur. It is, however, reasonable to suppose that *'ᵃrôn 'ᵉlōhîm* is the older title; on which see J. Maier, *Das altisraelitische Ladeheiligtum*, Berlin, 1965, p. 45.
32. *Die Überlieferung von der Thronnachfolge Davids*, Stuttgart, 1926.
33. Op. cit., pp. 4ff. His exact delimitation of the ark-source is as follows: 1 Sam. iv. 1*b*–18*a*, 19–21; v. 1–11*b*, 12; vi. 1–3*b*, 10–14, 16, 19 – vii. 1; 2 Sam. vi. 1–15, 17–20*a*.
34. Kosters, art. cit., pp. 361ff.; T. C. Vriezen, *Orient. Neer.*, 1948, pp. 174, 188; H. U. Nübel, *Davids Aufstieg in der Frühe der israelitischen Geschichtsschreibung* (diss.), Bonn, 1959, pp. 76ff.; Schunck, op. cit., pp. 97f.
35. E.g. R. A. Carlson, *David, the Chosen King*, Stockholm, 1964, pp. 58ff.
36. Bleek–Wellhausen, op. cit., pp. 208f.; M. Dibelius, *Die Lade Jahves*, Göttingen, 1906, pp. 20f.; W. Caspari, *Die Samuelbücher*, Leipzig, 1926, p. 460; Nowack, op. cit., pp. xxxiff.; de Vaux, *Les Livres de Samuel*, p. 167.
37. See N. H. Tur-Sinai, *V.T.*, i (1951), pp. 275ff.
38. The cultic aspects of 2 Sam. vi are represented in different ways by S. Mowinckel, *Psalmenstudien*, II, Kristiania, 1932, 81ff., 109f.; A. Bentzen, *J.B.L.*, lxvii (1948), pp. 37ff.; J. R. Porter, *J.T.S.*, N.S. v (1954), pp. 161ff.; H. J. Kraus, *Die Psalmen*, Neukirchen, 1961 (2nd end), p. 882; *Worship in Israel*, pp. 183ff.
39. See A. Weiser, *The Psalms*, London, 1962, p. 781; T. E. Fretheim, *J.B.L.*, lxxxvi (1967), pp. 296ff.
40. R. A. Carlson, op. cit., pp. 58ff., makes much of these stylistic indications.
41. As argued by Rost, op. cit., pp. 11f.; also accepted by C. Steuernagel, *Lehrbuch der Einleitung in das Alte Testament*, Göttingen, 1912, pp. 332ff.; Gressmann, op. cit., pp. 11ff., 233ff.
42. With Sam. Targum. See, *inter alios*, de Vaux, op. cit., p. 45.
43. See Tur-Sinai, art. cit., pp. 275ff.

44. The preposition can mean 'into' only if the ark is thought of as a container (e.g. Deut. x. 1), but it is certainly not so thought of here.
45. See Wellhausen, *Der Text der Bücher Samuelis*, Göttingen, 1893, p. 66. οὐκ ἠσμένισαν would correspond to *lō' ḥāḏû* or *lō' hērī'û*. Wellhausen, op. cit., p. 65, reads *lō' niqqû* and translates 'sie kamen nicht gut davon'. J. Bewer, *J.B.L.*, lvii (1938), pp. 89ff., turns it round the other way and reads 'the men of Beth-shemesh rejoiced but Yahweh did not rejoice in them' which seems forced and does not take account of LXX. Tur-Sinai, art. cit., pp. 275f., reads: 'and no one went unpunished in Yahweh's smiting'. He traces the textual confusion to the rare *nkn* which he also finds in 2 Sam. vi. 6 in what is generally taken to be a proper name, Nacon (cf. 1 Chron. xiii. 9, 'Kidon' meaning 'ruin').
46. Cf. Chenaniah charged with the transport of the ark in 1 Chron. xv. 27; also Chonaniah *et al.* Klostermann, op. cit., p. 21, suggests that Jeconiah was a Levite.
47. Names formed with *'ōz* (*Uzz-*) occur frequently in Benjaminite and Levitical lists and this word has a strong thematic association with the ark, e.g. Ps. lxxviii. 61; cxxxii. 8 = 2 Chron. vi. 41; see G. Henton Davies, in *Promise and Fulfilment* (*S. H. Hooke Volume*), Edinburgh, 1963, pp. 51ff. In some psalm texts *'ōz* may refer to the heavenly fortress or citadel of which the ark is the earthly counterpart, e.g. Ps. viii. 3; lxxviii. 26; cxxxii. 8; cl. 1.
48. Presupposing the identity of Beth- and Ir-shemesh which may be deduced from a comparison of 1 Kings iv. 9 with Joshua xix. 41. See Alt, *K.S.*, II, 282, n. 5; Abel, *Géographie de la Palestine*, II, 282, 343; Aharoni, *The Land of the Bible*, pp. 214, 287.
49. Rather than to the time of Josiah as defended by Alt, *K.S.*, II, 276ff.; Noth, *Das Buch Josua*, p. 93. For the earlier date see Aharoni, op. cit., pp. 265ff.; *P.E.Q.*, xc (1958), pp. 27ff.; Kallai-Kleinmann, *V.T.*, xi (1961), pp. 223f.; H. Tadmer, *I.E.J.*, xi (1961), pp. 143ff.; B. Mazar, *I.E.J.*, x (1960), pp. 65ff. There is no reason why pre-monarchical tradition could not have been incorporated in these lists.
50. Albright, in *Louis Ginzberg Volume*, New York, 1945, pp. 49ff.; Aharoni, op. cit., pp. 269ff.; H. Cazelles, *P.E.Q.*, lxxxvii (1955), p. 171.
51. Judges xviii. 30f. Judges v. 17 seems to imply that the migration took place before the decisive battle of Taanach, and Gen. xlix. 16f. and Deut. xxxiii. 22 also suggest the conclusion that by the time of composition Dan had moved north. Nothing certain can be concluded from the Samson cycle of narratives (though see Alt, *K.S.*, I, 161).
52. See E. Grant and G. E. Wright, *Ain Shems Excavations*, Haverford, Pa., 1931–9; F. M. Cross and G. E. Wright, *J.B.L.*, lxxv (1956), pp. 215f.; W. F. Albright, *A.A.S.O.R.*, xxi–xxii (1943), pp. 5f.; G. E. Wright, *B.A.*, xviii (1955), p. 57; J. A. Emerton, in *Archaeology and Old Testament Study*, pp. 197–206.
53. See J. Dus, *Comm. Viat.*, vi (1963), pp. 61ff.
54. On the Danite sanctuary and priesthood see G. W. Ahlström, *Aspects of Syncretism in Israelite Religion*, pp. 25ff.; A. Fernandez, *Bib.*, xv (1934), pp. 237ff. C. Hauret, in *Mélanges bibliques rédigés en l'honneur de André Robert*, Paris, 1957, pp. 105ff.
55. 2 Kings xvii. 23; xxv. 21; Jer. lii. 27; iii. 1; Amos v. 5.
56. Aharoni, op. cit., pp. 286f.
57. In *Judges* the duration of the period of affliction is generally stated followed by the Israelite *revanche* (iii. 8; vi. 1; x. 8; xiii. 1).
58. Cf. the Deuteronomic passages Judges vi. 6–10 and x. 10–16. In discussing the passages dealing with the ark in 1–2 Sam. we should bear in mind the role of the Levites in Deut. and the Deuteronomist history.

59. Confirmed by the occurrence of *bᵉnê yiśrā'ēl* in 1 Sam. vii. 6–8, found also in the Mizpah-strand of Judges xx–xxi. Caspari, *Die Samuelbücher*, Leipzig, 1926, p. 81, speaks of a Mizpah-narrator in 1 Sam. vii. 2ff.
60. See pp. 53f. This judgement affects particularly the presentation of Samuel as 'judge' and his role in the war with the Philistines. The Philistines were not subdued for the rest of Samuel's lifetime (see ix. 16; x. 5; xiii–xiv) and Saul not Samuel was responsible for their discomfiting. See J. Wellhausen, *Prolegomena zur Geschichte Israels* (6th edn), 1927, pp. 258ff.; Nowack, op. cit., pp. 31f.; Kennedy, *I and II Samuel*, Edinburgh, 1905, p. 68; C. A. Simpson, *J.S.S.*, iv (1959), p. 108; A. Weiser, *Z.T.K.*, lvi (1959), p. 270 *et al.* For a stereotype time-span of twenty years cf. Judges xv. 20; xvi. 31; 1 Sam. iv. 18 (LXX).
61. Wellhausen, *Die Composition des Hexateuchs und der historischen Bücher des Alten Testaments* (3rd edn), Berlin, 1899, p. 242.
62. E. Dhorme, *Les Livres de Samuel*, Paris, 1910, p. 69, regards the water libation, the milk lamb and the thunder of Yahweh as original i.e. belonging to a genuinely ancient tradition. Noth, *Überlieferungsgeschichtliche Studien*, p. 60, n. 2, posits a pre-Deuteronomic Mizpah tradition. It is clear, however, that the Deuteronomists edited early material in the light of their own specific religious presuppositions.
63. Cf. 1 Sam. vii. 7 with 2 Sam. v. 17. Both narratives refer to the miraculous and theophanic assistance of Yahweh, both conclude with an aetiological etymology. Stylistically 1 Sam. vii. 13 is close to 2 Sam. v. 22 (cf. vi. 1).
64. Cf. 2 Sam. xxi. 15–17; xxiii. 8–17. For stylistic analysis of these Philistine war episodes see Blenkinsopp, *J.B.L.*, lxxxii (1963), pp. 65ff.; *C.B.Q.*, xxvi (1964), pp. 427ff.
65. Theophanic and miraculous occurrences are elsewhere frequently associated with the ark and the ark is closely associated with the Holy War. See F. M. Cross, in *Biblical Motifs: Origin and Transformations* (ed. A. Altmann), Cambridge, Mass., 1966, pp. 11ff.; D. R. Hillers, *C.B.Q.*, xxx (1968), p. 49.
66. Cf. 1 Chron. xiv. 16, LXX[BA] and Isa. xxviii. 21. Accepted by Wellhausen, *Der Text der Bücher Samuelis*, p. 166; Thenius–Löhr, op. cit., p. 138; Caspari, op. cit., p. 459; Budde, op. cit., p. 226; de Vaux, op. cit., p. 167 *et al.* S. R. Driver, *Notes on the Hebrew Text and the Topography of the Books of Samuel*, p. 265, retains M.T. on the grounds of topography.
67. Cf. Isa. xxviii. 21 where Perazim and the valley of Gibeon are mentioned together. There are good grounds for identifying the valleys of Rephaim and Gibeon. See G. A. Smith, *The Historical Geography of the Holy Land* (25th edn), London, 1931, p. 218; Alt, *K.S.*, I, 200; de Vaux, op. cit., p. 166; Aharoni, op. cit., p. 260; id., *P.E.Q.*, xc (1958), pp. 27ff.
68. Introductory *'ōḏ* appear in 2 Sam. xxi. 15, 18, 19, 20. For the most part, these events take place in the same locality.
69. See the commentaries and a recent discussion in my article in *J.B.L.*, lxxxviii (1969), pp. 146, 150ff.
70. The term *ba'ᵃlê yᵉhûḏāh* is of a type found elsewhere in the Old Testament; cf. Judges ix. 2 etc.; 2 Sam. xxi. 12; Num. xxi. 28. LXX[B] has ἀπὸ τῶν ἀρχόντων, Aqu. and Symm. ἐχόντων (i.e. burghers).
71. The 'house' of Micah (Judges xvii. 8, 12) seems to be identical with the *bêṯ 'ᵉlōhîm* in verse 5 and Micah too, like Abinadab, appointed his son as the resident priest. The 'house' of Dagon was certainly a temple. However, the reference to Jeroboam making 'houses on the high places' in 1 Kings xii. 31 would suggest a distinction between these shrines and large cult-centres such as those at Bethel and Dan.
72. The names Abinadab and Eleazar invite comparison with the names of

Aaron's sons Nadab and Eleazar and are of a kind frequently associated with the Levitical cultic service (e.g. Exod. viii.6; x.23; 1 Kings iv.14; 1 Chron. vi.7; viii.30; ix.36; xxiii.21). In this connection we should recall that Gibeon is one of the cities 'given to the descendants of Aaron the priest' (Joshua xx.13, 17). Both names have parallels in the cognate languages (e.g. Akk. *Abu-nadib, Ili-haziri*; Ugar. gentilic *ndbn, bn ndbn*) and are probably theophoric.

73. See 1 Sam. xvi.8; 1 Chron. ii.13; also Amminadab, Ruth iv.19; 1 Chron. ii. 9f. See p. 86.

74. It is certainly not a place-name, cf. LXX[B] ἐν τῷ βουνῷ; see Budde, op. cit., p. 46; Klostermann, op. cit., p. 22; de Vaux, op. cit., p. 45, *et al.* Porter, art. cit., p. 169, translates 'in the hill', representing Yahweh imprisoned like Baal or Marduk in the mountain.

75. We omit the phrase 'on every green hill' occurring frequently in a homiletic context in the Deuteronomic corpus. The occurrences are as follows: (i) Exod. xvii.9, in the account of Moses' victory over the Ammonites which has some interesting points of resemblance with Joshua x.10–14 – the magical or quasi-magical action, insertion of a poetic fragment, the role of Joshua with Hur (cf. 2 Chron. i.5), the completion of the victory before sunset (xvii.12; cf. Joshua x.13*b*). See Bentzen, *Introduction to the Old Testament*, London, 1962, pp. 141f. (ii) Joshua v. 3, *giḇ'āṯ hā'ᵃrālôṯ*, in or near Gilgal where the Gibeonite treaty took place. Since the reason given for the circumcision of Israelites at this point is far from convincing, as the commentators generally agree, it may be suggested that this circumcision ceremony, like that of the Shechemites in Gen. xxxiv.13ff., accompanied a treaty between Israelites and non-Israelite settlers. The Hivite Gibeonites would, presumably, not have been circumcised. (iii) Judges vii.1, the 'hill of Moreh', of unknown location. (iv) 2 Sam. ii.24, the 'hill of Ammah' is described in the M.T. as being 'on the way to the wilderness of Gibeon'.

76. The phrase *har YHWH* occurs only here and in Num. x.33, in a context dealing with the ark, and in Gen. xxii.14 where some scholars have seen a connection with the ritual execution of the Saulites (see p. 124, n. 25).

77. 1 Kings iii.3ff.; 2 Chron. i.3ff.

78. 1 Chron. iii.5f. contains two introductions to the procession narrative in which the starting point is referred to as: Kiriath-jearim, Baalah, Kiriath-jearim which belongs to Judah. Reference to Baalah with the accompanying gloss is an interesting conflation of Joshua xv.9*b* ('Baalah, that is, Kiriath-jearim') and xviii.14 ('Kiriath-baal, that is, Kiriath-jearim, a city belonging to the tribe of Judah'). This shows that the Chronicler had no independent authority of his own for this assertion.

79. Bethel and Dan were also rivals to Jerusalem as Gibeon had been. See J. Gray, *I & II Kings*, London, 1963, pp. 288ff.

80. See *J.B.L.*, lxxxviii (1969), pp. 153–6.

81. *ha'ᵃlû* (vi. 21) and *wayya'ᵃlû* (vii. 1) imply a procession; cf. 1 Kings xii.28, 30. That Ekron, Beth-shemesh and Kiriath-jearim are all boundary points (Joshua xv.9–11) may suggest an early ark-procession round tribal boundaries as proposed by E. Nielsen, *S.V.T.*, vii (1960), p. 63, but this is uncertain.

82. *J.B.L.*, lxxxviii (1969), pp. 153ff.

## NOTES TO CHAPTER VII (pp. 84–97)

1. David was one of several 'Hebrews' who fought alongside the Philistines and their allies (see 1 Sam. xiv.21; xxix.3); it was only the mistrust of some

Philistine captains which prevented him from taking part in the decisive action against Saul.

2. See p. 61. That a treaty was confirmed between David and the Gileadites is further suggested by the adhesion of Barzillai (2 Sam. xvii.27; xix.31–40; note the recurrence of the term *ḥesed* in 1 Kings ii.7).
3. In 2 Sam. xix.20 Shimei ben-Gera the Benjaminite says that he is the first of all the house of Joseph to greet the king.
4. See Eissfeldt, 'The Hebrew Kingdom', *C.A.H.*, II, ch. XXXIV, pp. 44f. Noth, *The History of Israel*, pp. 187f., holds that Jerusalem was taken later than the events recorded in 2 Sam. v.17–25. Our impression is that 2 Sam. v.17–25 comes from an episodic history of the Philistine wars (or of the wars of David in general) which is continued in viii. 1ff. and excerpts from which can be found in the 'appendices' to Sam. in 2 Sam. xxi–xxiv. That vi.1–19 is placed after the summary account of victories in v.17–25 suggests that the ark could be moved only after the Philistines had been driven from the Gibeonite region. It may be noteworthy that the Chronicler places the two victories between the two phases of the transference of the ark: from Kiriath-jearim to the house of Obed-edom, from the house of Obed-edom to Jerusalem (1 Chron. xiii–xv).
5. 1 Sam. xxi.1ff.; 2 Sam. viii.17f.; xx.25f. The reference in this last text to a priest of David called Ira the Jairite is of interest here since LXX translates *hy'ri* ὁ Ιαρειν, the form used elsewhere (e.g. Joshua ix.17) for -jearim. Another Ira, one of the 'Thirty', is an Ithrite and the Ithrites are a Kiriath-jearim clan according to the Chronicler (see 2 Sam. xxiii.38; 1 Chron. ii.53).
6. For the place-names Gederah and Gedor see pp. 5f.
7. On the Chronicler's genealogies in 1 Chron. i–iv see J. M. Myers, *I Chronicles*, Garden City, N.Y., 1965, pp. 6ff.; Noth, *Z.D.P.V.*, lv (1932), pp. 97ff. Other relevant texts are: 1 Sam. xvi.1ff.; 2 Sam. iii.2–5; v.13–16; Ruth i.1–5; iv.13–22. David was most at home in the Negeb south of Hebron inhabited by Kenites, Kenizzites and other groups associated with Judahites, see especially 1 Sam. xxiii.14ff.; xxvii.8ff. He came to settle in Hebron, a Calebite city inhabited previously by non-Semitic groups (see Judges i.10, 20 etc.). Both the previous name of this city and that of Ziklag are non-Semitic, probably Hurrian. The Moabitic element in his descent attested in Ruth iv.17–22 may find support in 1 Sam. xxii.3–4 and would not be ruled out by his later conquest of that country (2 Sam. viii.2). On the question of ethnic affinity with Kiriath-jearim groups see *J.B.L.*, lxviii (1969), pp. 153ff.
8. See 2 Sam. iii.2–5 and v.14–16 for the names of his sons. We cannot help noting the prevalence of theophoric names with -el: Eliab, Daniel (1 Chron. iii.1), Elishua, Elishama, Eliada, Eliphelet. Other theophoric elements may be implied in Solomon and Abshalom, Elishua (cf. Bathshua, 1 Chron. iii.5) and Abinadab (1 Sam. xvi.8). Nor can this possibility be ruled out for the name David, on which see J. J. Stamm, *S.V.T.*, vii (1960), pp. 165ff.
9. Cf. the meeting between Johanan and Ishmael 'at the great waters which are in Gibeon' (Jer. xli.12). It will be recalled that Gibeon was one of the cities occupied during Sheshonk's (Shishak's) campaign ca. 924 B.C. On the basis of his ordering of the list Aharoni, op. cit., p. 287, concludes not unreasonably that the negotiations referred to in 1 Kings xiv.25–8 would have taken place at Gibeon.
10. *yāṣā*, suggests a military campaign; see Eissfeldt, *La Nouvelle Clio*, iii (1951), pp. 110ff., and *Kleine Schriften*, III, Tübingen, 1966, 132ff.
11. See Eissfeldt, *Kleine Schriften*, III, 132; Y. Yadin, *J.P.O.S.*, xxi (1941), pp. 110–16; R. de Vaux, *Bib.*, xl (1959), pp. 495ff.
12. See pp. 63f.

13. See pp. 6f.
14. For Israelite–Philistine relations in general at this time see Noth, *The History of Israel*, pp. 182ff., and Eissfeldt, *The Hebrew Kingdom*, pp. 42ff.
15. See Smith, op. cit., p. 273; S. R. Driver, op. cit., p. 188; de Vaux, *Les Livres de Samuel*, p. 154. For *'ammāh* in post-biblical Hebrew see M. Jastrow, *A Dictionary of the Targumin, the Talmud Babli and Yerushalmi, and the Midrashic Literature*, London and New York, 1903, p. 75. Presuming a location near Gibeon, the pursuit could not have lasted very long.
16. See pp. 61f. The Chronicler's Gibeonite 'genealogy', which includes that of Saul, implies an ethnic association between peoples in Gibeon and Maacah (1 Chron. viii. 29ff.).
17. Ed. C. C. Torrey, *The Lives of the Prophets* (J.B.L. Monograph Series, vol. 1), Philadelphia, 1946, p. 30. That a case is made out in the oracle against building a temple in Jerusalem may, if this information is historical, be explained by the Gibeonite provenance of Nathan. According to G. Ahlström, *V.T.*, xi (1961), pp. 113ff., Nathan belonged to a Jebusite party which opposed the building of the temple.
18. See pp. 101ff.
19. See J. Wellhausen, *Die Composition des Hexateuchs und der historischen Bücher des Alten Testaments*, pp. 260ff.; M. Noth, *Überlieferungsgeschichtliche Studien*, p. 62; Eissfeldt, *The Old Testament. An Introduction*, pp. 242f. The appendices are arranged in a dual formation set out chiastically: xxi. 1–14; xxiv (three years' famine, three days' pestilence); xxi. 15–22; xxiii. 8–39 (lists of warriors and their feats); xxii; xxiii. 1–7 (verse compositions attributed to or dealing with David).
20. Noth, op. cit., p. 62; Eissfeldt, op. cit., p. 324; Budde, *Die Bücher Samuel*, pp. 304, 313ff.
21. More probably prior to this since David's treatment of the seven Saulites seems to provide an explanation of his attitude to Mephibaal, especially in view of the question in ix. 1. In this case the positive exclusion of Mephibaal in xxi. 7 would have to be interpreted as a clarification introduced when the narrative was displaced.
22. Other examples of this link-formula are: 2 Sam. ii. 1; viii. 1; ix. 1; x. 1; xiii. 1; xv. 1; xxi. 18. See J. Schildenberger, *Studia Anselmiana*, xxvii–xxviii (1951), pp. 142ff.; J. Blenkinsopp, *S.V.T.*, xv (1965), pp. 46f.
23. This genre has been studied particularly by Gressmann and Sellin. R. Pfeiffer, *Introduction to the Old Testament*, New York, 1948, p. 353, reads xxi. 1–14 as one of a series of political acts carried out by David in the name of piety. The designation of 'saga', used by Eissfeldt (op. cit., p. 281 – 'sagenhaft' in the original), seems appropriate only to the last part of the narrative which tells of the vigil of Rizpah.
24. Rizpah and Aiah, verse 10.
25. xxi. 1–14 probably comes before ix. 1ff., and xxiv after it. See Eissfeldt, *Die Composition der Samuelbücher*, Leipzig, 1931, p. 53; H. Gressmann, *Die älteste Geschichtsschreibung und Prophetie Israels* (2nd edn), Göttingen, 1921, pp. 141ff.
26. Noth, *The History of Israel*, p. 192; Eissfeldt, *The Hebrew Kingdom*, p. 48; Bright, *A History of Israel*, p. 180; Albright, *Archaeology and the Religion of Israel*, p. 120; Alt, *K.S.*, II, 50–2.
27. A Hurrian origin for this name was proposed many years ago by several scholars including Landersdörfer, Brögelmann and Sayce; see the last-named in *J.T.S.*, xxii (1921), pp. 267f. More recently this has been argued by W. Feiler, *Z.A.*, xlv (1939), pp. 222f. H. B. Rosén, *V.T.*, v (1955), pp. 319f., proposed a Hittite origin.

28. Several scholars argue that Zadok and other cultic officials of David were formerly Jebusite; see in particular H. H. Rowley, *J.B.L.*, lviii (1939), pp. 113ff.; *Festschrift für Alfred Bertholet*, Tübingen, 1950, pp. 461ff. Some aspects of temple-worship may go back to pre-Israelite Jebusite practice, though here scholarly assessments differ widely, cf. de Vaux, *Ancient Israel*, pp. 309ff., with Ahlström, op. cit., pp. 34ff.
29. For Canaanite influence on the Hebrew monarchy in general see J. Gray, *The Legacy of Canaan* (2nd edn), Leiden, 1965, pp. 218ff., and for David in particular A. Kapelrud, *Z.A.W.*, lxvii (1955), pp. 200f.; B. Maisler (Mazar), *B.J.P.E.S.*, xiii (1947), pp. 105ff.; S. Yeivin, *V.T.*, iii (1953), pp. 149ff.
30. See Albright, in *Louis Ginzberg Volume*, New York, 1945, pp. 49ff.; Aharoni, op. cit., pp. 269ff., with further bibliography. It is noteworthy that these cities are situated in the most 'Canaanite' parts of the country, see H. Cazelles, *P.E.Q.*, lxxxvii (1955), pp. 171f.
31. On the practice of blood-vengeance see Exod. xxi.24; Deut. xix.21*b*; Num. xxxv.33; Gen. ix.5f. The negotiations have to be seen within this context as noted, for example, by E. Merz, *Die Blutrache bei den Israeliten*, 1916, p. 24; J. Pedersen, *Israel I–II*, London and Copenhagen, 1926, pp. 384f.; J. van der Ploeg, *C.B.Q.*, xiii (1951), p. 301, but we must not forget that the Gibeonites explicitly reject this alternative ('neither is it for us to put any man to death in Israel', verse 4, where *bᵉyiśrā'ēl* has a precise technical sense; cf. 2 Sam. xiii.12).
32. See pp. 20ff.
33. Assimilation would have been decisively advanced by the administrative reforms of Solomon, referred to earlier, and his conscription of non-Israelite populations for forced labour. On the latter see M. Haran, *V.T.*, xi (1961), p. 161.
34. 2 Kings iii.27 provides a comparison. The King of Moab sacrificed his son on the wall of besieged Kir-hareseth with the result that 'great wrath' came upon the Israelite army which was forced to retire.
35. See Schunck, op. cit., p. 107, n. 170. It may be worth noting at this point that historical passages dealing with Gibeon evince some interesting similarities with narratives generally attributed to the Elohist in the Pentateuch. Thus, the points of contact between Joshua ix and Deut., commented on in an earlier chapter, cannot adequately be explained simply by Deuteronomist editing. Many of the older commentators have noted affinities between the battle narrative in Joshua x and certain E passages which speak of the miraculous intervention of God, and the quotation from the Book of Yashar may also suggest an Elohist context (see S. Mowinckel, *Z.A.W.*, liii (1935), pp. 130ff.). Most scholars attribute the earliest Pentateuchal texts dealing with the ark to E, especially Num. xiv.44, and the Elohist's predilection for dreams is well known (cf. 1 Kings iii.5; 2 Sam. vii.4, cf. Ps. lxxxix.20). The parallel narratives 2 Sam. xxi.1–14 and xxiv.1–25 have identical *excipits* except that the former is 'Elohist' and the latter 'Yahwist'. The parallelism is continued in revelations to Solomon first at Gibeon (1 Kings iii.4ff.) then at Jerusalem (ix.1–9). This suggestion cannot be pursued further here, but it would seem worth examining more thoroughly the possibility that a Gibeon–Mizpah tradition, preserved fragmentarily in Judges and Sam., has contributed to the formation of the so-called Elohist strand in the Pentateuch. This would also, incidentally, add interest to the similarities, pointed out earlier, between Gen. xxii and Num. xxv.1–5, generally attributed to the Elohist, and 2 Sam. xxi.1–14.
36. J. Gray, *The Legacy of Canaan* (2nd edn), Leiden, 1965, p. 126, n. 1; H.

Cazelles, art. cit., pp. 165ff.; A. Kapelrud, *Z.A.W.*, lxvii (1955), pp. 198ff.; *Suppl. Numen*, IV, Leiden, 1959, 294ff.; J. Prado, *Sefarad*, xiv (1954), pp. 43ff.; R. Dussaud, *Les origines canaanéenes du sacrifice Israélite* (2nd edn), Paris, 1941, pp. 287ff.

37. See Gray, op. cit., pp. 20ff.; T. Worden, *V.T.*, iii (1953), pp. 292f.; U. Cassuto, *I.E.J.*, xii (1962), pp. 77ff. We presume that the bodies of the Saulites were exposed until the autumn rains as against Hertzberg, op. cit., p. 384, who takes verse 10 to refer to early rainfall in late spring or the beginning of summer.
38. See texts in Cazelles, art. cit., pp. 167f.
39. See Worden, art. cit., pp. 283, 287; Ginsberg–Maisler (Mazar), *J.P.O.S.*, xiv (1934), p. 247.
40. See E. Dhorme, *R.B.*, vi (1909), p. 53; D. J. Wiseman, in *Archaeology and Old Testament Study*, p. 130, for evidence from the Tušratta letter and Alalakh personal names for ŠMŠ-worship among Hurrians. A Hurrian text from Mari refers to a sacrifice in honour of *[d]Dagan ša ḫur-ri*; see I. Gelb, *Hurrians and Subarians*, Chicago, 1944, p. 63. From Judges xvi. 23 we see that the Philistines had also made Dagan their god.
41. As does H. Bardtke, *T.L.Z.*, lxxxv (1958), col. 106.
42. An obvious example is Gen. iv. 11f. See Pedersen, op. cit., pp. 384f.; R. Patai, *H.U.C.A.*, xiv (1939), pp. 267f.
43. J. B. Pritchard, *Gibeon where the Sun stood still*, p. 120.
44. See 2 Sam. vi. 17; vii. 2; xi. 11; xv. 24–9.
45. M. Görg, *Das Zelt der Begegnung*, Bonn, 1967, pp. 128ff. The same suggestion had been made many years earlier by E. Sellin, *Einleitung in das Alte Testament*, Leipzig, 1910, p. 15.
46. For the literary analysis of the passage see J. Gray, *I & II Kings*, pp. 117–23, and other commentaries ad loc. W. Staerk, *Z.A.W.*, lv (1937), pp. 29f., derives it not from D but from a genuinely ancient tradition not convinced of the legitimacy of Jerusalem.
47. See Cazelles, *S.V.T.*, iii (1955), pp. 26ff.; J. A. Soggin, *Z.A.W.*, lxxviii (1966), pp. 189f.
48. See Noth, *S.V.T.*, iii (1955), pp. 225ff.; A. van den Born, *Koningen*, Roermond, 1958, p. 32; J. Gray, op. cit., p. 119.
49. Gray, op. cit., p. 123.
50. This would lead us to look once again at the description of Gibeon as 'like one of the royal cities', *k[e]'aḥat 'ārē hammamlākāh* (Joshua x. 2). The only other occurrence of this phrase is 1 Sam. xxvii. 5 referring to the capital city of the Philistine king Achish as opposed to 'country towns'. Amos vii. 13 speaks of Bethel as a 'royal sanctuary', *bêṯ hammamlākāh*, implying that it was the national shrine of the Northern Kingdom. This might lead us to read 2 Sam. vi as the account of the transference of the political and religious capital from Gibeon to Jerusalem.
51. See in particular G. von Rad, *Old Testament Theology*, I, 41; S. Herrmann, *Wissenschaftliche Zeitschrift der K. Marx-Universität*, Leipzig, 1/3 (1953/4), pp. 51ff.; A. Malamat, *B.A.*, xxi (1958), pp. 96ff.; Alt, *V.T.*, i (1951), pp. 21f.
52. *A.N.E.T.*, p. 499.
53. J. B. Pritchard, *The Bronze Age Cemetery at Gibeon*, Philadelphia, 1963, pp. 32, 156.
54. See especially in Keret and Aqhat, texts in Driver, *Canaanite Myths and Legends*, Edinburgh, 1956, pp. 28ff., 48ff.
55. This seems to have first been suggested by A. B. Ehrlich; see J. Lindblom, *H.U.C.A.*, xxxii (1961), p. 104, and J. Gray, *The Legacy of Canaan*, p. 210.

56. See most recently Rowley, *Worship in Ancient Israel*, pp. 74ff. I have not had access to S. Yeivin, *Revue d'Hist. Juive en Égypte*, i (1947), pp. 143ff., suggesting that the prayer was addressed to a wisdom-deity.

## NOTES TO CHAPTER VIII (pp. 98–108)

1. For a recent discussion of this text see Aharoni, op. cit., pp. 283–90.
2. Hananiah's encounter with Jeremiah probably took place ca. 594 B.C. For the names see p. 1.
3. Ezra ii.20 M.T. has Gibbar (*gbr*) for Gibeon in Neh. vii.25. Ezra ii.25 reads Kiriatharim, omitting *yod*. In view of the associations between Kiriath-jearim and Bethlehem, alluded to earlier, we may note that Bethlehem and Netophah, together with two Benjaminite cities, occur between Gibeon and the other Gibeonite cities.
4. See pp. 12f.
5. xx.1, 3; xxi.1, 5, 8. See commentaries ad loc. and Eissfeldt, 'Der geschichtliche Hintergrund von Gibeas Schandtat (Richter 19–21)', in *Kleine Schriften*, II, Tübingen, 1963, 64–80.
6. 1 Sam. vii.2–14; x.17–27; possibly xii. In vii.16 Mizpah is one of the places at which Samuel judged.
7. In favour of Tell en-Naṣbeh is the modern name itself and its position on the road north from Jerusalem. If, however, Asa's action was defensive there would be no need to choose a site on the northern boundary of Judah, and Ramah, the other city fortified by him, is some distance south of Tell en-Naṣbeh. But the most serious difficulty against Tell en-Naṣbeh is that the city-gate faced north not south. This does not mean that this identification is ruled out but rather that it cannot be accepted unconditionally until these difficulties are cleared up.
8. Israelite occupation is not seriously attested at Tell en-Naṣbeh until after the United Monarchy. See J. Muilenburg, *I.D.B.*, III, 407–9; D. Diringer, in *Archaeology and Old Testament Study*, pp. 329ff.; de Vaux, *Les Livres de Samuel*, p. 47.
9. See p. 111, n. 50.
10. As pointed out by Albright, *A.A.S.O.R.*, iv (1922/3), p. 93.
11. To suppose that this was a circuitous route known only to Ishmael or that the meeting was planned to take place at Gibeon are hypotheses not supported by the text. See J. Bright, *Jeremiah*, Garden City, N.Y., 1965, p. 255.
12. On the use of κατέναντι in LXX see Hatch and Redpath, *A Concordance to the Septuagint and the Other Greek Versions of the Old Testament*, II, Oxford, 1895–7, 749. Dalman, *P.J.B.*, vii (1911), pp. 14f., proposed Joshua iii.16 as illustrating a wider usage, but Jericho (Tell es-Sultân) is less than six miles from the Jordan and, in any case, the preposition here is ἀπέναντι. For the situation of Nebi Samwil see H. Vincent, *R.B.*, xxxi (1922), pp. 360ff.
13. This is a further case of 1 Sam. vii.2–14 influencing the tradition on the early cultic history of Israel.
14. The basic cause of confusion was the name itself, designating a common topographical feature in Palestine. It may be added that both Alt and Albright identified Tell en-Naṣbeh with biblical Ataroth *and* with the Mizpah fortified by Asa; see Alt, *Z.D.P.V.*, lxix (1953), pp. 1ff.; Albright, *A.A.S.O.R.*, iv (1922/3), pp. 33ff.
15. The former is probably a pre-Israelite, the latter an Israelite formation. See Isserlin, *P.E.Q.*, lxxxix (1957), pp. 133ff.
16. We find no mention of Gibeon and Gibeonites in passages usually attributed

to P, with the possible exception of a Priestly redaction of Joshua ix, on which see p. 34f.

17. Also 1 Sam. ii.22*b*, though this may be a late gloss based on Exod. xxxviii.8, as suggested by Wellhausen, Budde *et al.* See H. P. Smith, op. cit., p. 20.
18. See most recently H. H. Rowley, *Worship in Ancient Israel*, pp. 50f., and for P's cultic concepts in general von Rad, *Die Priesterschrift im Hexateuch*, *B.W.A.N.T.*, IV, 13 (1934); also *Gesammelte Studien zum Alten Testament*, Munich, 1958, pp. 109ff. (E.Tr.: *The Problem of the Hexateuch and Other Essays*, Edinburgh and London, 1966, pp. 103–24); K. Koch, *Die Priesterschrift von Ex. 25 bis Lev. 16*, Göttingen, 1959.
19. Ps. xv.1; xxvii.5; lxi.4; Isa. xxxiii.20; Jer. x.20; Lam. ii.4; Ezek. xli.1. As is clear from cognate languages, especially Arabic, Ethiopic and Akkadian, *'hl* has the primary connotation of settlement, habitation or the like. This may provide a semantic basis for the association, often attested, between sanctuary and social or political unit, e.g. Ps. lxxviii.67f. This is supported by the frequent occurrence of *mškn(t)* in Hebrew and Ugaritic in apposition to *'hl.*
20. 1 Sam. i. 7, 9, 24; iii.3. A Rabbinical tradition contained in M.Zeb. xiv.6 has attempted to combine both tent and temple by supposing that the walls of the Shiloh sanctuary were of stone and the roof of tent cloth. See Ahlström, op. cit., p. 29.
21. See Rowley, op. cit., pp. 51, 79, and further references in n. 2.
22. G. von Rad, *Old Testament Theology*, I, 348, n. 3.
23. See especially 1 Chron. xiii–xvii. Von Rad, op. cit., pp. 350ff.
24. Infringement of the ritual prescription that the ark must be borne by Levites, 1 Chron. xv.2.
25. E. L. Curtis and A. A. Madsen, *The Books of Chronicles*, Edinburgh, 1910, pp. 315f.; A. C. Welch, *The Work of the Chronicler*, London, 1939, pp. 31ff.; W. A. L. Elmsie, *Interpreter's Bible*, III, New York and Nashville, 1954, 403f.; J. M. Myers, *II Chronicles*, Garden City, N.Y., 1965, p. 6; von Rad, *Old Testament Theology*, I, 238, n. 114, *et al.* Against this view see the recent contribution of M. Görg, op. cit., pp. 121–4.
26. The tent, the house of the tent, the house of Yahweh (1 Chron. ix.19–23), the dwelling (*miškan*) of Yahweh (xvi. 39), tent of meeting (*'ōhel mô'ēd*) (xxiii. 32), the dwelling of the tent of meeting (vi. 17 [M.T.]) and some other variations of these.
27. As some have suggested, there may be a confusion here between the tent at Gibeon and that pitched by David in Jerusalem; but the Chronicler probably thought of Solomon bringing the Mosaic tent directly from Gibeon. See Myers, *II Chronicles*, p. 28.
28. It is by no means impossible that the introduction of cultic music and the establishment of temple singers, no doubt based on Canaanite models, goes back to David.
29. See 1 Chron. xvi.37–42; xxi.29; xxiii.32; 2 Chron. i.5f.
30. That Zadok was associated with Gibeon is also widely doubted or denied. For the Jebusite origins of Zadok see S. Mowinckel, *Ezra den Skriftlärde*, Oslo, 1916, p. 109; A. Bentzen, *Z.A.W.*, li (1933), pp. 173ff.; H. H. Rowley, *J.B.L.*, lviii (1939), pp. 113ff.; *Bertholet Festschrift*, Tübingen, 1950, pp. 461ff.; *Worship in Ancient Israel*, pp. 73f. Other contributions to the question deserving mention are: K. Budde, *Z.A.W.*, lii (1934), p. 49; H. G. Judge, *J.T.S.*, N.S. vii (1956), pp. 70ff.; Ahlström, op. cit., pp. 123ff.; C. E. Hauer, *J.B.L.*, lxxxii (1963), pp. 89ff. We may add that the position taken by the Chronicler has at least as much in its favour as the Jebusite hypothesis, especially in view of the close religious and cultural ties between Gibeon and Jerusalem in the early period.

31. See p. 132, n. 72.
32. It seems that the prohibiting angel of 1 Chron. xxi.29f. cannot be dissociated from the destroying angel propitiated by the sacrifice on Araunah's threshing floor (2 Sam. xxiv.16ff.). Taken together, these two fragmentary narratives point back to a theological rationale of the transference of the royal cultic centre from Gibeon to Jerusalem.
33. Zeb. 118*b*. This and the following quotations and references are from *The Babylonian Talmud*, ed. I. Epstein, London, 1935.
34. Zeb. 118*a*–119*a*.
35. Shiloh, Nob, Gibeon is the usual order but we also find Nob, Gibeon, Shiloh (Yoma 67*b*), Gibeon, Shiloh (Meg. 9*b*, Soṭah 16*a*), Gilgal, Nob-Gibeon, Shiloh (Zeb. 118*a*).
36. Zeb. 61*b*.
37. From a targum on 1 Chron. xvi.39. See Rowley, op. cit., p. 213.
38. See E. Auerbach, *Wüste und gelobtes Land*, 1, Berlin, 1936, 90f.; Hertzberg, *Z.A.W.*, xlvii (1929), p. 176; Sellin, *Gilgal*, pp. 45, 91; M. Haran, *Judah and Jerusalem* (in Hebrew), Jerusalem, 1957, pp. 38f.
39. Priests (ix.10–13), Levites (verses 14–16), gatekeepers (verses 17–27), in charge of sacred utensils (verses 28–32), Levitical singers (verses 33f.), descendants of Gibeonites (verses 35–44).
40. Curtis and Madsen, op. cit., p. 169; Myers, op. cit., pp. 67ff.
41. Apart from 1 Chron. ix.2 only in Ezra ii.43, 58, 70; vii.7; viii.17, 20; Neh. iii.26, 31; vii.46, 60, 73; x.28 (M.T. verse 29); xi.3, 21.
42. I. Mendelsohn, *B.A.S.O.R.*, lxxxv (1942), p. 14.
43. Reference to 'the people of Israel' in Joshua ix.17f., 26 and the '*ēḏāh* in verses 18f., 21 suggest a liturgical view of the community; cf. 'Israel' as a term for the laity in Ezra ii.2 etc. and the priestly connotations of the term '*ēḏāh*.
44. Ezra ii.70; vii.7; Neh. vii.73; x.28.
45. See p. 34.
46. 1 Kings ix.20. This may well explain 'the sons of Solomon's servants' in Neh. xi.3 and vii.46, 57 (=Ezra ii.58) who were closely associated with the *nethinim*. See M. Haran, *V.T.*, xi (1961), pp. 159ff., and for a somewhat different view B. A. Levine, *J.B.L.*, lxxxii (1963), pp. 207ff. Other relevant comments may be found in Mendelsohn, art. cit., pp. 14ff.; id., *B.A.S.O.R.*, clxvii (1962), pp. 31ff.; *Slavery in the Ancient East*, New York, 1949, pp. 92ff.; A. Biram, *Tarbiz*, xxiii (1952), pp. 137ff.
47. Ezek. xliv.6f. Rowley, op. cit., p. 100, understands these to be temple guards but there are good analogies for foreigners serving in a menial capacity in temple activities.
48. See 2 Chron. ii.17f.; viii.7f.; 1 Chron. xx.3.
49. Yeb. 71*a*, 78*b*–79*a*; Hor. 4*b*; Mak. 13*a*. Num. xxxi.30, 47, with its reference to Moses and Eleazar 'giving' them to the Levites, may reflect the use of this term already in existence rather than explain its origin. Comparison has been suggested with Ugaritic *ytnm* which appears to designate a class. See Myers, *Ezra. Nehemiah*, Garden City, N.Y., 1965, p. 19.
50. Yeb. 79*a*; Abod. Zar. 27*a*; Hor. 4*b*.
51. See p. 133, n. 75.
52. Bek. 45*b*.

# INDEX OF BIBLICAL REFERENCES

# GENERAL INDEX